Smiles over Coffee

INSPIRATIONAL STORIES, QUOTES, AND QUIPS ABOUT FRIENDSHIP

Mary Hollingsworth
GENERAL EDITOR

Guideposts Books
CARMEL, NEW YORK

Editorial, research, and content development managed by Shady Oaks Studio, Bedford, Texas. Team members: Patty Crowley, Vicki Graham, Rhonda Hogan, Mary Hollingsworth, Sue Ann Jones, Mary Kay Knox, Kathryn Murray, Nancy Norris, Stephany Stevens, Stephanie Terry, and Barbara Tork.

Produced in association with Mark Sweeney & Associates, Bonita Springs, Florida.

www.guideposts.org
(800) 431-2344
Guideposts Books & Inspirational Media Division
Designed by Cindy LaBreacht
Cover by Lookout Design Group
Typeset by Inside Out Design & Typesetting

Printed in the United States of America

Contents

Introduction

"Friendship is the golden thread that ties the heart of all the world," said John Evelyn. It's the glue that holds everything together. It cements relationships between children, marriage partners, families, communities, and even nations. When friendship is missing, so is joy, peace, and love.

Friendship can take on a variety of images. It may look like romance, as it did with Anthony and Cleopatra. It may look like comedy, as it did with Lucy and Ethel. And it may look like commitment, as it did with Jonathan and David. Whatever personality it takes on, friendship is surely at its core.

Smiles over Coffee gives us delightful glimpses of friendship at its finest . . . and funniest. So pour yourself a cup of coffee and be prepared to smile your way through these hilarious and touching pages.

Let There Be Laughter! is a series of books created with one purpose in mind—to brighten your spirit, lighten your load, and give you delightful moments of restorative laughter. We at Guideposts assembled a team to look high and low for funny and wholesome writings that celebrate the lighter side of living. This series is the result of their research. And we hope you have as much fun reading it as they did putting it together.

You'll find stories relating hilarious, real-life tales; rib-tickling jokes and cartoons; absurd, frozen-moment-in-time anecdotes; top-ten lists and other miscellaneous grin getters; great quotations that make you smile; and some of the best one-liners we've ever seen.

God gave us laughter! And believe it, He knew what He was doing. Because we wish you a dose of healthy fun and inspiration, we give you this book. In the midst of your day-to-day life, may it bring a smile to your face and true joy to your heart.

Let there be laughter!

The Editors

What made us friends in the long ago

when first we met?

Well, I think I know;

the best in me and the best in you

hailed each other

because they knew that

always and always

since life began

our being friends was part of God's plan.

GEORGE WEBSTER DOUGLAS

1

Friendship Frivolity

Friendship is fun. In fact, it can be downright hilarious at times. Funny happenings are twice as funny when shared with your best friend. And sad times are only half as sad.

ALL ROADS LEAD TO TEXARKANA

Now, for the most part, I'm pretty together. At least that's what my friends tell me. I'm an organization freak. I don't forget too many things, I don't usually lose things, and I'm fairly punctual and on top of my appointments. My clothes match, except on an occasional Saturday when I don't care. I go to the hairdresser to stay presentable to the rest of the world. And my car is as tidy as a little old lady's who only drives it to church on Sundays . . . hmmm. My clothes are hanging together in color families in my closet, and I even fold my lingerie and keep it neatly arranged in boxes in my dresser. (OK, so I'm a little over the top on the neat-freak meter.)

Actually, all that "together" description is what made this story seem quite strange to my friends at the time.

A few years ago, my best friend, Charlotte, and I decided to take a few days of R&R in Hot Springs, Arkansas, while she was on spring break from school. You know, the whole hot-mineral-baths-and-massage routine. So we left the Dallas-Fort Worth metroplex and drove about halfway, where we stopped at my parents' home in Sulphur Springs, Texas, to spend the night. That helped break up the trip and gave us a chance to see my folks.

The next morning, before we left for Hot Springs, we asked my dad for the shortest route from Sulphur Springs to Hot Springs (it was a "springy" trip). And he gave us specific directions, which he said should take about three hours. Instead of going through Texarkana on Interstate 30, he suggested we go north on Highway 19 across the Red River and then take highway 71 east into Hot Springs. So away we went.

Since Charlotte is not a morning person, I volunteered to drive first. And because we'd had eggs for breakfast, which Charlotte was allergic to, about the time we crossed the Red River she fell asleep. No problem! I was wide awake and had been up Highway 19 many times before, since I grew up in that part of East Texas.

We'd been driving about two hours, Charlotte snoozing away all the time, when she roused. What you have to know about Charlotte is that she has this built-in radar device in her brain. Even if she's asleep, if you start traveling in the wrong direction, she feels it and wakes up. She never gets lost, and if she's ever been to a place once, she can go back without any map or directions. It's plain spooky . . . especially for someone like me.

The thing is, Charlotte hadn't really traveled with me very much at that point, so she didn't *know* that when God handed out *compasses,* I thought he said *"rumpuses,"* so I asked for a very small one, and he gave me the smallest one he could find.

In other words, if I go into a store at the mall, when I come out I can't remember which way I was going when I went in. Or if you make two turns, I'm lost (sometimes just one turn will do it). I can even get confused going to my office (that's probably not funny until you realize I work at home). I'm the poster child for directionally dysfunctional people. I can't find my way somewhere with a map, two hands, and flashlight.

"Where are we?" Charlotte asked as she sat up.

"We're still going north on Highway 19," I said confidently.

"Then why are we crossing the Red River *again* and that sign up there says it's 21 miles to Texarkana?"

"Well, I don't know," I said defensively. "I haven't made one single turn since we got onto Highway 19 in Sulphur Springs. I've just been watching for Highway 71 to Hot Springs."

"You must have turned somewhere, because we're definitely going south, not north."

"I did *not.*"

"Well, maybe the road split and you took the wrong fork in the road."

"Did *not.*"

"Hmmm. Well, all I can say is we're going the opposite direction we should be going. So let's look at the map. Pull over."

I pulled into an old, deserted gas station and stopped. Charlotte got out the map and studied it for a minute. Then her shoulders started shaking, and she began laughing.

"What's so funny?" I asked with some irritation.

"Well, friend, we've made a grand circle, and we're almost back where we started."

"No way!"

"Yes, way . . . way *out* of the way, in fact."

"Well, I'm not very good at directions."

"No kidding!" she laughed. "Next time I'd better drive."

"Drive! You couldn't even stay awake."

Then we both got tickled as we compared dysfunctions and came up even.

We decided it would be faster to just go on to Texarkana and take I-30 into Hot Springs, instead of turning around. So that's what we did. And instead of our trip taking three hours, it took five hours. When we arrived, we really *needed* a hot bath and massage.

The joke among my friends (at least *they* think it's funny) is that whenever Mary drives you end up in Texarkana, no matter where you intended to go. (Bunch of cynics! Some friends they are.)

Mary Hollingsworth

....

In the sweetness of friendship let there be laughter, and sharing of pleasures.

Kahil Gibran

....

THE *SOUND OF MUSIC* SURVEY

I've heard that friends must have enough common interests to get along well and enough differences to make things interesting. You know the song: "You like tomato and I like tomahto. . . ." That sure is the case with my friend Kimberlyn and me. We're both writers, have preteens, and are unconventional "midlife" moms. She loves quaint. I love quirk. She loves the romantic Victorian era and all things Beatrix Potter. She has even named her house Linden Cottage. I, on the other hand, am more of a "tomboy's woman." I like the distressed look of French Country and all things Sesame Street. I have also named my house: the Nut Haus. Recently, I suggested that we see just how different we were in certain areas. So we put on our Julie Andrews thinking caps, and with our best

Sound of Music savvy, wrote down a few of "our favorite things":

MUSIC
Kimberlyn: Classical, Pachelbel's "Canon"
Rachel: Country, "Did I Shave My Legs for This?"

KID'S BEDTIME STORY
Kimberlyn: *The Secret Garden*
Rachel: *Elmo Has a Boo-Boo*

KID'S BIRTHDAY PARTY
Kimberlyn: Tea party at the Ritz-Carlton
Rachel: Mr. Cheesy's Pizza Parlor

BRUNCH SPOT
Kimberlyn: The Blue Owl Tea Room
Rachel: The Donut Place

BOOK
Kimberlyn: Jane Austen's *Pride and Prejudice*
Rachel: *The Complete Idiot's Guide to Organizing Your Life*

DEVOTIONAL BOOK
Kimberlyn: Oswald Chambers's *My Utmost for His Highest* (in the original, archaic language, of course!)
Rachel: Emilie Barnes's *Fifteen Minutes Alone with God*

Although Kimberlyn has more refined tastes, we enjoy each other's company and have learned a good deal in the process. For example, after talking to her, I realized that my favorite classical piece was in fact called Pachelbel's "Canon" and not Taco Bell's "Canon." And I also learned that the purists do not consider doughnuts a pastry. Kimberlyn says that they are in a food group alone—ditto for pork cracklins. She's learned a few things from me, too. Namely, that "ain't" is the primary compound verb that holds a good country song together and that you can buy a *Complete Idiot's Guide* to just about anything under the sun. She commented, "That title sounds patronizing to me." I replied, "What's patronizing mean?"

Isn't it great how friends can expand each other's horizons? Good friends with whom we have much in common— as well as those with many differences—can keep us from getting stuck in a rut, provide a new perspective when we face a tough decision, and help us laugh when we feel like crying. Simply put, friends can double our joy and halve our sorrow.

Why not grab a friend and conduct an informal *Sound of Music* survey of your own? Don't be surprised if one of you bursts into an operatic rendition of "Climb Every Mountain" while the other yodels her way through "The Lonely Goatherd." That's okay. *Vive la difference!* You might be surprised by the fascinating things you learn or at least have some good laughs at some of your *Odd Couple* idiosyncrasies.

Rachel St. John-Gilbert

When Perfect Isn't Enough

I went through my address book, calling each of my friends and passing on all of my faithful instruction. Here's what I told them:

Unless you want it to come out your nose, don't laugh and drink soda at the same time.

No matter how bad the flea problem, don't spray Raid on your dog. Sure the fleas will come right up to the surface all nice and dead, but your dog will start making funny sounds like the time your cousin Steve got a piece of pretzel stuck in his right tonsil and kept making those disgusting hacking noises while you were all trying to watch *The Wizard of Oz,* and your Aunt Rita kept yelling at your Uncle Al, "See, I told you we shoulda had his tonsils out."

Mayonnaise makes great hair conditioner. However, if you wrap your mayonnaisey head in plastic while you sleep, your body heat will turn the mayo rancid.

Don't believe anyone who tells you that drinking a cup of vinegar a day will melt away your fat. All it does is make you feel like a pickle from the inside out and cause your breath to smell like a jar of gherkins.

Remember where you park, especially at Disney World, where they name their parking places after Disney characters. Nothing's worse than walking around the Disney lot thinking you're "Happy" when, in fact, you're Dopey."

Don't let your car know when you have some extra money. Same thing goes for your furnace, water heater, and septic tank.

No matter what the diet books say, when you're craving a Snickers candy bar, munching carrot sticks doesn't satisfy—unless you dip them in hot fudge and roll them in chopped, salted peanuts. Even then you have to wash them down with chocolate milk.

If you have a choice between taking out the trash or letting it sit down in the basement and forgetting about it until it produces more maggots than you thought ever existed on earth—choose taking out the trash.

Don't shop for bathing suits with anyone whose hips are smaller than yours.

Unless you like a dull finish, don't wash your car with bleach. Neither should you use bleach for washing out your fishbowl, unless you like your pet fish floating belly-side up. Do, however, use bleach to remove mildew from the shower, but don't forget to wipe your feet off before you run on your dark gray carpeting to answer the phone (unless you like the look of white footprints down the hall).

Nancy Kennedy

The best mirror is an old friend.

George Herbert

LAUGHING AT YOURSELF

I've read Winnie-the-Pooh stories, but I'd never known anyone who had a personality just like Eeyore until I met Marlene. She amazes me with her ability to see disaster or a dark cloud behind every possible moment in life. Here are actual conversations I've had with Marlene over the years:

(1987) "I'm getting married, Marlene."

"Well, you know it's not all it's cracked up to be."

(1996) "We're going to have a baby, Marlene."

"Well, your life is over."

(2002) "We're getting a pool, Marlene."

"Oh, dear God, someone will drown for sure."

Once, after a particularly grueling fifteen minutes of talking to Marlene, in which she had found something negative to say about one hundred issues I'd run through, I stopped and said to her, "Marlene, at least in heaven everything will be good."

"What?" she said.

"Heaven," I said. "At least in heaven everything will be perfect."

Marlene paused as if thinking and then she said, "Sure. In the beginning."

Now, my pet peeve is negativity. I am convinced Marlene has some kind of a genetic predisposition to see the dark in this world where others see light. So what is it about her that makes me appreciate her as a friend? I'll tell you. It's because she can laugh at herself. There is a great deal to be said for someone who can laugh at herself.

For the thirty years I've known Marlene, I have played back her conversations for her, and she has, without exception, been able to see the humor in them. She can't change. She's been trying to be more positive for the entire time I've known her. Her efforts to be positive are even funnier because she will say something positive with a negative twist: "The sun is shining today. It's the first sun we've seen in days," or, "Sure, our sons are on the honor roll, but that just means an expensive college education."

But Marlene also has the ability to laugh at herself. There is humility in the ability to laugh at yourself. Laughing at yourself can be an acquired art. It takes practice. It involves not taking yourself too seriously. Try it. Even if you are just like Marlene, without the humor part. Try it. You'll be shocked at the good it will do you.

Marsha Marks

CRAZY FOR COCOA PUFFS

L ast week a friend of mine said, "You should meet Susan. She's really disciplined about what she eats. She's so disciplined she even puts padlocks on her fridge and pantry so she doesn't eat anything fattening."

I hate to burst anyone's bubble here, but Susan is NOT disciplined. A better word to describe Susan would be "creatively impaired." This is because any woman in the throes of a binge—any woman with an ounce of imagination, that is—would not be deterred for a heartbeat by the presence of a mere padlock on the freezer door. Nosiree.

A lock means nothing. It's kind of like wearing a T-shirt onto the floor of an Amway convention that says, "No. Please. Stop. Whatever you do, DON'T tell me how I can achieve financial freedom AND be my own boss without ever leaving the comfort of my living room."

I figure, when it comes to the mood to binge, where there's a will there's a way. For example, if MY fridge were padlocked, I'd head for my kids' stash of Halloween candy. If all the good candy happened to be gone, I'd reach for my car keys. And if for some reason I wasn't able to find the keys to my car, no problem.

Ever see a woman rumbling into a Dairy Queen on a riding mower?

Sometimes a woman's gotta do what a woman's gotta do.

Padlock on the fridge? C'mon. Give me a REAL hurdle. Something with teeth.

I have other addictions, too. Junk food isn't the only one. The other thing I'm addicted to is mail order catalogs. I get so many catalogs that two years ago my mailman canceled his gym membership, and his forearms still look like Popeye's. There's so much processed pulp around my house that my address is listed in the National Directory of Forests and Forestry.

> **Ever see a woman rumbling into a Dairy Queen on a riding mower?**

But that's all. Just junk food and junk mail. Everything else in my life has some sort of redemptive value. Well, okay, almost everything, except for all those mindless TV shows I love. But that's it, I promise. Just junk food, junk mail, and junk TV.

Which is okay, right? I mean, it's just entertainment, right? So my figure is about as curvaceous as a Twinkie. I'm starting to believe I deserve all those catalog offerings I covet, and I've practiced for so long that I can watch TV for hours now without even the slightest twinge of conscience.

But it's all in fun.

Right?

Of course, when it comes to binging on junk food, it's easy to know when I've overdone it. My scale, body shape, energy level, and even my blue jeans don't hesitate to scold me when I get too far out of line!

But what about those other binges? What about when I've binged on head candy—when I've filled my brain with ideas or images that are materialistic or hedonistic, when I've lusted after lifestyles or laughed at plot lines promoting values I don't embrace. What happens then?

It's so easy to get desensitized.

Several years ago, my friend Cherie Spurlock taped an index card above her TV. On it were these words, taken from Philippians 4:8 (KJV): "Whatsoever things are true, whatsoever things are honest, whatsoever things are just, whatsoever things are pure, whatsoever things are lovely, whatsoever things are of good report; if there be any virtue; and if there be any praise, think on these things."

If I took that verse to heart, I'd definitely want to cut back on the head candy, those nutrition-free binges of input that fatten up my sin nature and leave my spirit clogged and lethargic.

Maybe this wouldn't be a bad subject to bring up with family and friends. Maybe we could encourage each other to think about what we put into our brains. Maybe we could talk about making healthier choices. Maybe we could even figure out how to take that verse from Philippians and make it come alive in our own daily walks.

I think these would be great conversations to have.

I think they'd be even greater if we had them over root beer floats. Meet me at Dairy Queen. I'll be the one on the John Deere.

Karen Scalf Linamen

SPLASH OF COFFEE IN YOUR MILK?

Supposedly a true story. Ian works in a coffee, bagels, and sandwiches trailer on the campus of The University of New Hampshire. Vinnie is his boss and the owner. According to Ian, the following exchange actually happened (Ian is telling the story):

Her: Yes, I'd like a milk with some coffee in it.

Me: So, that's just a splash of coffee in a milk?

Her: No, a regular amount of milk, but not coffee.

Me: Is there more milk or coffee?

Her: Oh, definitely more coffee.

Me: So that's a coffee with some extra milk.

Her: Just the usual amount of milk.

Me: A coffee with milk.

Her: Yes.

Me: Anything else?

Her: A little extra milk and do you have coffee with no caffeine?

Me: We do have decaf.

Her: No, I don't want decaf, just some coffee without the caffeine.

Me: Ma'am, that's what decaf means: no caffeine.

Her: Oh, then do you have milk with no caffeine?

Me: Milk doesn't come with caffeine.

Her: Yes it does.

Me: Not that I know of; where do you get your milk?

Her: It doesn't say caffeine free on the milk so it must have caffeine.

Me: Oh, you're right, my mistake, I forgot that we only get the decaf milk. No problem, we have only decaf milk. Anything else?

Her: Do you have any bagels?

Vinnie: (who has been listening all along): I'm sorry, ma'am we're all out of decaf bagels.

Her: Well, what are those? (pointing at sesame bagels)

Vinnie: Those are sesame donuts with extra caffeine added.

Her: I guess I'll just have the coffee.

Her: Do you take credit cards?

Me: No, ma'am, cash only.

Her: What about Visa?

Me: Is that a credit card?

Her: Well, yes.

Vinnie: Is it cash?

Her: No.

Vinnie: Then no, we can't take it.

Her: What about checks?

Me: Cash ma'am, nothing else.

Her: O.K.

Her: How much is that?

Vinnie: Eleven dollars and forty-five cents.

Her: Really?

Vinnie: New war in Alaska is ruining the coffee business, plus you wanted the coffee with no caffeine, that's hard to find now, had to grow it myself.

Her: O.K. (proceeds to write a check)

Vinnie: Please leave.

Her: Why?

Vinnie: You're raising my blood pressure, leave now.

Her: But what about my coffee?

Vinnie: Leave and never return.

She leaves, but pays the $11.45 first. Seriously.

Clean Funnies

LONG LOST FRIENDS

It happens in almost every house:

The phone rings and you hear the voice of some friend, relative (or friend of a friend or relative) so long lost you grope to place the identity. "Why—why, how wonderful," you exclaim. "Where are you?"

And as they admit they are either in the city or approaching it, "Gracious, we'd just love to see you"—even as you make frantic calculations: How many beds can we make up? Did those towels get back from the laundry? "You—you must come out for dinner." And as they demur that they wouldn't want to put you to any trouble, you not only insist, you find yourself urging that they spend the night. No, no, it won't put you out a bit, you won't do a *thing.*

Hanging up, you gaze wildly about the tumbled house. And food! You can hardly feed them the intended leftovers and it's too late to thaw a roast; you'll have to go to the store. Meanwhile, you start barking orders: "Pat, go clean up your room, they'll have to sleep there—you can have the couch. Freddy, put those puzzles away and sweep the rug. Janey, go out in the yard with Jimmy and see if you can find enough dry branches to start a fire. Also, anything that remotely resembles flowers. Now hurry, everybody, they should be here in an hour."

And you go galloping off to the grocery intent only on steak for supper, bacon for breakfast, lettuce, some rolls—and spend twenty dollars. And there's a long line before the cashier, it takes longer than you thought; and as you finally come panting into the homestretch, you see, with sinking heart, the out-of-state car.

They've found a shortcut, they announce triumphantly over the kisses and exclamations—here they are!

And the fireplace that should be blazing brightly is stone cold. Janey comes in with three frostbitten, bedraggled weeds. The sweeper's dead center of the rug while Freddy gazes transfixed at the TV set. And why, oh why didn't you at least put on a skirt before going to the store?

But, still frowsy and frenzied, you strive to be the cordial hostess even as you stash some groceries away, snatch out others. And if your husband is going to have all these relatives why can't he get home and help entertain them? And thank goodness here he is to make the fire and mix the drinks and bolster conversation while you get dinner on.

And between courses you slip to the basement to check the sheets and signal a daughter to iron them before the evening's over, hoping she doesn't get the one with the mended place in the middle. And where did you put those thick bright Christmas-present towels?

And you sit up late visiting, showing home movies, getting acquainted or reacquainted, and there is a sense of fellow-ship, of warmth and goodness and drawing together that compensates for the confusion. And when at last you are all bedded down you whisper to your husband, "They're really lovely, aren't they? I'm really glad they came."

And in the morning you linger over a fresh pot of coffee after the children are off to school. You find yourself urging, "You don't have to go on today, do you? Can't we show you around?" And when the hearty thanks and farewells have been said, you wave at the departing car with a curious sense of loss. "Good-bye, good-bye, come back soon!" you call—and mean it.

It's been worth all the trouble.

Marjorie Holmes

SELFLESS LOVE

Friendship. There's something so special about that word.

The world bows to people who have so committed them-selves to each other.

In honor of friendship, wars have been fought and won, for-tunes have been given away, crowns have been relinquished.

In service to friendship we stand vigil at the bedside of the dying, adopt orphans, care for widows, and clothe the needy. Friendship brings warmth to a shivering beggar, company to the lonely, and laughter to the hurting.

In commitment to friendship, men and woman have been burned at the stake, torn apart by lions, maimed, imprisoned, and martyred.

In tribute to friendship, symphonies have been composed, classics written, and masterpieces painted.

It is a word of respect and awe, a word of prayer and hope. It is love in its rarest, most selfless form . . . friendship.

Mary Hollingsworth

· ·

WITH FRIENDS LIKE THESE

One of the most delightful weekends I had spent since moving to California six months before was nearing an end. Two teenage girls approached me while I was counting out my vitamins. "What are all those pills for?" one of them asked. "Well," I explained, "these two are for beautiful eyes, this one is for long willowy legs, that little one is for pearly, white teeth . . ." and as I was waxing on, the other girl interrupted me with, "Haven't been taking them long, have you?"

Luci Swindoll

He deserves paradise who makes his companions laugh.

Horace

· ·

TRUE FRIENDSHIP

Whatever happened to friendship that really meant something? You know, the cross-your-heart-and-hope-to-die kind of friendship. It seems we've lost it somewhere between the lunar landing and "Fantasy Island." Remember the kinds of friends we grew up with? The ones who lived on the pages of our favorite books? They were real friends—friends who knew what it was to sacrifice, endure, and triumph.

Take those wonderful characters in A. A. Milne's books: Piglet, Eeyore, Tigger, Winnie-the-Pooh, and all the rest. They didn't run out on one another if things were going badly. They didn't sit and gossip or berate each other. This is not to say they didn't disagree—they often did. But they talked things out. They endured one another's weaknesses with encouragement and support. When Pooh, having consumed way too much honey during a visit with Rabbit, got stuck in the doorway on the way out, did all his friends lecture him on the evils of overindulgence? Did they counsel him and cart him off to a weight-loss clinic for obese bears? Of course not. They sat by his side and read stories to him for a whole week until he had thinned down enough to be yanked out. Real friends don't applaud your pitfalls. They help you recover gracefully and then let you figure out the lesson yourself!

Friends care. Would Raggedy Ann say, "C'est la vie" if she knew a friend was lost or depressed? Definitely not. Somewhere, deep in her candy heart, lived a concern for even the least of the playroom population. The dented tin dog was just as precious as the priceless porcelain princess. Raggedy Ann had a heart for others. Her cotton-stuffing brain worked overtime planning ways to improve the lot of her friends. She cared little that her painted smile might fade in the rigors of her efforts, for even when things appeared most desperate, her shoe-button eyes never lost their sparkle of hope. Wouldn't you respond to a friend like that?

Or what about the delightful creatures in Kenneth Grahame's *Wind in the Willows*? Ratty was always gracious and willing to endure Mole's clumsy efforts without drawing undue attention to the latter's obvious lack of social graces. What a lovely quality for a friend to have. Certainly we've all be in a position where our *savoir-fare* was less than it should have been!

Perhaps what made Rat and Mole and Badger and Toad all so compatible was their unswerving devotion to animal etiquette. Mole cites, for example, that it is against animal etiquette to dwell on possible trouble ahead or to ever comment on the sudden disappearance of one's friends at any moment, for any reason or no reason whatsoever. Seems like that would certainly put a stop to the sort of meddling and backbiting that destroys so many contemporary friendships. Maybe what we need today is a good dose of animal etiquette!

One of the very best examples of true friendship, however, is found between the covers of E. B. White's children's classic, *Charlotte's Web*. Who could ever forget those unlikely, yet devoted friends. Wilbur, the simple, bumbling pig and that great intellectual, Charlotte the spider? Did Charlotte use her superior intellect to lord it over Wilbur? I should say not. They were neighbors and therefore friends. And there's a lesson for us all. It didn't matter to Charlotte that Wilbur could never return a favor in like kind. She was a giver, that spider. And with her final ounce of energy and her last centimeter of silk, she saved the life of her friend. There's the sacrificial kind of friendship that doesn't come neatly packaged. It takes plain hard work to be a friend like Charlotte.

Wouldn't it be wonderful to have friends like these today: a Pooh Bear to cheer us, a Raggedy Ann to care for us, a Ratty to patiently teach us, and a Charlotte to rescue us! Yet perhaps it would be better still to be a friend like these.

Pamela Kennedy

* * *

The best time to make friends is before you need them.

Ethel Barrymore

* * *

BITS AND PIECES

Bits and pieces.

Bits and pieces.

People. People important to you. People unimportant to you cross your life, touch it with love, and move on. There are people who leave you, and you breathe a sigh of relief and wonder why you ever came in contact with them. There are people who leave you, and you breathe a sigh of remorse and wonder why they had to go and leave such a gaping hole.

Children leave parents. Friends leave friends. Acquaintances move on. People change homes. People grow apart. Enemies hate and move on. Friends love and move on. You think of the many who have moved into your hazy memory. You look at those present and wonder.

I believe in God's master plan in lives. He moves people in and out of each other's lives, and each leaves his mark on the other. You find you are made up of bits and pieces of all who ever touched your life, and you are more because of it, and you would be less if they had not touched you.

Pray God that you accept the bits and pieces in humility, and wonder, and never question, and never regret.

Bits and pieces.

Bits and pieces.

Author Unknown

....

Friends are God's apology for relatives.

Hugh Kingsmill

....

"Oh, stop worrying—I told you,
he promised to bring you his best friend."

A FRIEND IN NEED NEEDS A FRIEND, INDEED

I'll never forget the day I made The Phone Call.

Stressed out by an overabundance of diapers, deadlines, and dirty dishes in my life, I was feeling under siege. Anxious. Overwhelmed. And so, looking for comfort, I did the only thing I could think of at the moment.

I went to the kitchen.

Ten minutes later I picked up the phone and dialed the phone number of bosom buddy Linda Holland. As soon as she answered, I found myself blurting my woes into the receiver.

"Help!" I cried. "I've just eaten an entire box of Cap'n Crunch!"

I knew my friend was a kindred spirit—a sympathetic soul who had "been there, done that"—when she immediately answered, "Ouch! Do you know what that'll do to the roof of your mouth?"

How did she know? Firsthand experience, no doubt.

When life gets a little rough, Cap'n Crunch is a stopgap measure. A temporary fix. A short-term solution. Chocolate is another short-term solution. Now I'll be the first to admit that eating chocolate doesn't produce lacerations on the roof of your mouth like and entire box of Cap'n Crunch has been known to do, but eating chocolate has its own set of disparaging side effects. Just ask my bathroom scale. On second thought, don't ask my scale. It has been privy to dark secrets even my husband will never know, and I'd just as soon keep it that way.

My point is that there are plenty of quick fixes around, things we can do that make us feel better for, oh, about a nanosecond until guilt or regret sets in. And those post-binge pounds aren't exactly a picnic, either.

And yet, in a world of quick fixes, we have alternatives. I'd like to talk about one of those alternatives in particular. It lasts longer than a box of Milk Duds. Nourishes better than a Twinkie. Has less calories than a Milky Way Lite. And is easier on the palate than Cap'n Crunch.

It's called friendship.

When we're feeling stressed, we tend to reach for the food. Maybe we should reach for the phone instead.

Button, Button, Who's Got the Button?

I've been blessed with some really wonderful friends. You and I have lots of people in our lives, don't we? Colleagues, acquaintances, neighbors . . . people who share our pew, carpool our kids, and type memos for our husbands. But every now and then someone crosses the line. They stop being an acquaintance or colleague and become a true friend.

When do you know someone has graduated to the status of being a true friend?

- When she can show up on your doorstep unannounced and your first thought isn't about yesterday's breakfast dishes in your kitchen sink.

- When you can stop in the middle of a sentence and say, "Am I whining?" and she knows you well enough to say "Yes."
- When you come home from work and find a note on your kitchen counter that says, "Couldn't find my can opener, so I let myself in and borrowed yours."
- When she says, "How are you doing?" and you know she really wants to know.
- When she'll tell you about the lipstick on your teeth or spinach at your gum line.

I think my friend Nancy Rottmeyer crossed a line into new friendship territory the day she came over and helped me paint and wallpaper my kitchen. The significance of this act of friendship takes on new meaning when you realize that Nancy and her husband, Larry, had just finished *paying professionals* to paint and wallpaper several rooms in their home. Trust me when I say that this fact did not go unnoticed by Nancy's husband when our two families met for pizza that night. His tongue-in-cheek observation ("Let me get this straight. Wallpapering our house was just too much work, but you wallpapered Karen's kitchen *just for fun?"*) made me appreciate Nancy's assistance all the more.

My friend Cherie Spurlock drops in for a visit, whips up some soapy water, and does my dishes while we chat. I called her house the other night at ten thirty, desperate for a blank videotape for a project I needed to finish before morning. After looking around, she came back on the line and said casually, "Nope. I don't have one. But tell me what kind you need and I'll run down to the supermarket and pick something up." I was moved by her generous offer, but told her I couldn't let her do that. Then she volunteered the services of her seventeen-year-old son. Now there was an offer I couldn't refuse!

How do you know someone's a true friend? There's something about that "extra" mile that says volumes. Yet sometimes it's not so much what a friend *does* as what she *perceives*.

When I became pregnant with Kacie, I had a hard time feeling any joy or excitement about my pregnancy, despite the fact that it was a long-awaited event. I know that my caution stemmed from a miscarriage several years earlier. What if I lost this baby, too? Maybe it was safer to postpone my excitement several months, until I could be certain this baby would survive.

That's when a bouquet of spring flowers arrived at my door. The note, penned by my friend Linda Holland, said, "Celebrate the new life within you!" And somehow, after her encouragement, I could.

Occasionally, however, something happens in a friendship that defies categorization. All you know for sure is that a mere acquaintance never would have risen to the occasion.

Like the day I went shopping with Beth Forester. The treasure I sought was a fancy blouse to wear to a glamorous dinner. Before long, I found the perfect blouse. And it was on clearance, too! The only problem was that it was missing two buttons.

Beth and I were standing together in my dressing room when she picked up an identical blouse, also on clearance, draped over a chair. "What's wrong with this one? It's not missing any buttons."

I sighed. "Wrong size."

And then we had an idea. As long as the store was going to have to sell a blouse with missing buttons, why shouldn't it be the blouse that didn't fit me? At my inquiry, an apathetic shrug from the dressing room attendant gave us the permission we needed. The problem was, we didn't have a pair of scissors or clippers with which to snip two buttons from the too-small blouse.

Beth raised the blouse to her teeth.

"There's one," she spit into her hand.

For the second button she resorted to her keys. She soon discovered that Buick keys saw through thread faster than keys associated with, say, Saturns or Chevys.

I wore my blouse the next evening. And what an evening

it was! One of my books was up for an award, and I felt gorgeous and confident in my new outfit. And even though the Gold Medallion went to someone else, the evening was magical. *Pillow Talk* was one of five finalists in its category. The music was heavenly. The speaker, dynamic. The food, rich and sumptuous.

That was eight months ago. This morning I walked into my closet and spotted the blouse I wore to the banquet. And when I did, the memories came flooding back, and I had to laugh.

You see, whenever I see that blouse, the thoughts that come to mind are not of candlelight and glory. Nah. I think of Beth, standing in the women's dressing room, biting the buttons off a clearance-rack treasure.

Now, that's a *true* friend.

Karen Scalf Linamen

ENTHUSIASM

Enthusiasm! It's the thrill of living life to the max. It's the highest peak in life's roller coaster ride—that point when you squeal with delight, and your stomach jumps up into your throat. It's the swish of skis on powdery snow, glistening bows on surprise packages, and the excited voice of your best friend.

Enthusiasm is the piccolo's trill in "Stars and Stripes Forever." It's the snaggle-toothed grin of a little boy holding a triple-dip ice cream cone. It's the standing ovation for the winner in the Special Olympics. Yes, it's the upside of life and the anticipation of things to come. And it's how our friendship makes me feel.

Mary Hollingsworth

••

Two doctors, who had been friends for many years, met on the street. Martin said, "Hi, Tom, you're fine . . . how am I?"

Author Unknown

••

THE EMPTY EGG

*H*e was nine, in a class of eight-year-olds. The third-graders did not welcome Philip to their group. He was *different*. He suffered from Down's Syndrome with all its obvious manifestations and its symptoms of retardation.

One Sunday near Easter, the Sunday school teacher poured a pile of plastic eggs that pull apart on the floor in front of the children. She told them that each child was to go outdoors the coming week and discover some symbol of "new life" and place that symbolic seed or leaf or whatever inside the egg. Then they would open their eggs one by one, and each youngster would explain how his find was a symbol of "new life."

The children gathered around her on the appointed Sunday and put their eggs on a table, and the teacher began to open them.

One child had found a flower. All the children "oohed" and "aahed" at the lovely symbol of new life.

In another egg was a butterfly. "Beautiful," the girls said. Another was opened to reveal a rock. Some of the children laughed.

"That's crazy," one said. "How's a rock supposed to be like a new life?"

Immediately a little boy spoke up and said, "That's mine. I knew everybody would get flowers and leaves and butterflies and all that stuff, so I got a rock to be different."

Eveyone laughed. The teacher opened the last one, and there was nothing inside.

"That's not fair," someone said. "That's stupid," said another.

The teacher felt a tug on her shirt. It was Philip. Looking up he said, "It's mine. I did it. It's empty. I have new life because *the tomb is empty!*"

The class fell silent.

From that day on, Philip became part of the group. They welcomed him. Whatever had made him different was never mentioned again.

Philip's family had known he would not live a long life; just too many things were wrong with his little body. That summer, overcome with infection, Philip died.

On the day of the funeral, nine eight-year-old boys and girls confronted the reality of death and marched up to the front of the church with their Sunday school teacher. Each placed on the casket of their friend their gift of love—not flowers, but an empty plastic egg.

Author Unknown

• •

Clara: **"When I get down in the dumps, I buy myself some new clothes."**

Sara: **"Oh, so that's where you get them."**

Rusty Wright & Linda Raney Wright

• •

WALLET, WALLET—WHO'S GOT THE WALLET?

Recently, I attended a business dinner at an out-of-town convention in Atlanta with some publishing colleagues.

A group of us shared a cab back to our respective hotels, and as we pulled up to the first hotel, I reached into my purse to get some money for the fare.

Problem was, earlier when I'd switched from my large day purse to my smaller evening purse, I hadn't had time to remove the essentials from my wallet. So, running late, I just jammed my thick, bulging-at-the-seams wallet into my slender evening purse.

Removing my too-big black wallet from my too-small black purse in a dark cab was like trying to pull my fresh-from-the-dryer too-tight   jeans up over my too-wide hips. While I was trying to yank my stubborn wallet from the confines of my purse, I was at the same time trying to hold up my end of a sparkling conversation with all my literary friends and colleagues.

Success at last!

My wallet was finally free from the stubborn clutch of the tiny black purse. By that time, however, someone else had already paid the full fare, so I promptly forgot about my wallet and focused my energies on making a good conversation impression instead.

Ten minutes later, I arrived at my destination where I was excited to catch up with some friends I hadn't seen in over a year. Only a couple members of our party had arrived, my friend Becky and a new friend, Lee, whom I'd just met earlier that day.

I joined them, and ordered a soft drink. When the waiter delivered it, I reached into my recalcitrant purse to pay and was pleasantly surprised to open it with nary a struggle.

That's when I discovered my wallet was missing.

Blind panic. Especially since I would have to fly home the next day and wouldn't have any ID.

Becky generously paid for my drink as I retraced my steps outside to where the cab had dropped me off.

No wallet.

I asked the valet parking attendants if a wallet had been turned in.

Nope.

Using Lee's cell phone, I called another friend, Chip, from the group who'd ridden in the cab with me to see if he'd found my wallet.

Nope again.

Then Lee donned his shining armor suit and with a little crafty Sherlock Holmes sleuthing helped me figure out the name of the cab company and put in a call to report the missing wallet.

By this time, the rest of our party had arrived, looking gorgeous, including my good friend Ellie. I looked a little less than gorgeous as I was perspiring profusely from a hot flash. Ellie kindly walked me back outside to the front of the hotel, praying all the way that the Lord would reveal the location of the missing wallet to us.

Nothing.

We returned to the others, and I decided I'd better go back to my hotel so I could call Michael and have him put a stop on all our credit cards.

W-a-a-a-h-h! Then I remembered I didn't even have any money to get back to the hotel! My friends passed the hat for me, and I started to stand up to leave.

Before I left, though, Donna, another new friend I'd just met that day, said, "Wait. Let's pray first." So, we all bowed our heads in the lobby of the Ritz Hotel in Atlanta while Donna loudly and fervently prayed, "Lord, you know where Laura is, and you know where that wallet is, and we know you can bring those two together. We trust you for the outcome. Amen."

I started to leave, and Lee's cell phone rang. As he answered it, he said, "Wait. This might be for you, Laura."

I looked at him skeptically and thought *Ri-ight* . . .

Lee began nodding and smiling into the phone, looking at me during the whole conversation. When he hung up, he did that guy thing of "YES-S-S!" where he made a fist and pulled it in to himself in exultation.

"That was Chip calling," he said. "Annette [another author friend who'd shared our cab] has your wallet."

I screamed

Laura Jensen Walker

••

Friendship doubles our joy and divides our grief.

Swedish Proverb

••

Promise Yourself

Promise yourself to be so strong that nothing can disturb your peace of mind.

To speak of health, happiness, and prosperity to every person that you meet.

To make all your friends aware of the special qualities within them.

To look at the sunny side of everything and let your optimism work to make your dreams come true.

To think, work for, and expect only the best.

To be just as enthusiastic about the success of others as you are about your own.

To forget past mistakes and press on towards a greater future.

To wear a cheerful countenance at all times, as a smile radiates warmth and love.

To give so much time to the improvement of yourself that you have no time left to criticize others.

To be too wise for worry, too tolerant for anger, and too courageous for fear.

To be happy.

Author Unknown

It's so much more friendly with two.

Piglet (in* Winnie-the-Pooh *by A. A. Milne)

A PLACE ALL TO MYSELF?

*H*urrying into my dorm room, I flung my books onto the jumble of papers on my desk. One more day till Christmas break. I was looking forward to going home, but even more I relished the prospect of coming back to a room all to myself. For the whole next semester I would have no roommate! I could practically taste the freedom.

Not that I didn't like my current roomie. Third-year music students at the university, we had gotten along well. But she was moving to a house off-campus, and after the semester I would be getting married. So for the time being, I could have quiet.

I got up and walked down the hall to the bathroom. Suddenly an all-too-familiar voice called from behind: "Lisa! Lisa!"

I turned in dismay. "Hi, Megan," I said, trying to be polite. "What are you doing up here?"

"I need to talk to you." Megan was a freshman music major who had grown annoyingly fond of me. She leaned close, flashing the grin that seemed never to leave her face.

"Sure," I said, backing away. Megan was always turning up at the least-opportune time. I didn't want to dislike her, but she was too overbearing.

"I'm looking for space in your dorm next semester," she said. "Do you know anyone whose roommate might be leaving?"

"No," I said, feigning sympathy. "I don't know anyone. I hope you find a place." I closed the bathroom door behind me.

Later that afternoon I went to the music building, where I had to make some fresh reeds for my oboe. That meant soaking a strip of new cane until it was pliant, tying it onto a cork tube, then scraping off the outer bark with a knife until it formed a reed of the right thickness that would vibrate properly. Normally I enjoyed whittling the cane. But I couldn't keep my mind on my task.

I kept thinking of Megan. Sooner or later she would find out I would be rooming by myself next semester. I hated having lied, but I couldn't bear giving up the privacy I desperately desired. And if she made me cringe during brief encounters, how would I possibly stand it day after day? Still, there had been a sense of urgency in her request that I couldn't get out of my mind.

I honed the knife on a whetstone, then scraped the reed carefully. I would be playing a solo for a holiday concert back home at my church. I needed a good reed. After pushing the cork into the top of my oboe, I put my lips against the reed and blew. Definitely too harsh. The reed was stiff.

I whittled some more, then blew again. Still not right. I

tried again, but couldn't get the distinctive tone that would indicate the reed was ready. As I continued, I tried not to let my frustration and tension creep into my hands; one nick could ruin the whole reed. But the more I tried to relax, the more harried I felt.

What's wrong, Lord? Why can't I do this?

The answer became clear. I was distracted by my own lack of suppleness. Unyielding and unresponsive, the reed was producing harsh sounds instead of sweet notes. It was just like my attitude toward Megan.

"Okay, God," I said, sighing. I put down the reed, then prayed, "Forgive me for lying to Megan and for having an unloving heart toward her. I want more than anything to do your will, so if you want me to invite her to live with me, I'll do it—"

I paused. How would I be able to tell whether or not it was God's plan? I continued: "God, if you want Megan to live with me, please show me by . . . by bringing her up to this very room and having her knock on the door." That seemed safe. This was one place where Megan had never followed me— and even if she happened to pass by, she wouldn't be able to see me because the window was covered with black paper.

Nonetheless, I hedged my bets. "One more thing, God. If she shows up and knocks and then sits in the chair beside me, I'll know for sure you want me to ask her."

I was confident I had requested the impossible. The reed room was tiny and crowded. The chair next to me held a toolbox and a stack of sheet music. I had never known anyone to sit on it.

Feeling more relaxed, I returned to my work. Within an hour I finished two reeds that sounded fine. I tucked them into my velvet-lined reed case and swept string and cane shavings into the wastebasket. It was nearing dinnertime, Megan was clearly nowhere nearby, and I began to visualize again the peace I would have living alone the next semester.

There was a knock on the door.

It can't be, I thought. I crossed the room and opened the door.

"Oh, you're in here," Megan said. "I was looking for somebody else."

"I was just leaving," I said weakly.

I watched in astonishment as she edged past me, moved the toolbox and sheet music to the table, and sat down in the chair. "I don't quite know what I'm doing here," she said.

I did. I was choked with surprise at having had my prayer answered so immediately and in such detailed fashion. "Megan," I said, "my roommate is moving out. If you like, you can move in with me next semester."

She threw her arms around me, then bolted out of the room. I could hear her running down the hall, shouting, "I'm moving in with Lisa next semester! Lisa said I could room with her!"

After Christmas break, Megan moved in. My previous roommate had been a casual person like me, comfortable in clutter; Megan kept her desk and bureau orderly, which made me attend to mine instead of letting it slip into chaos.

Living with me, Megan no longer needed to strive for my attention. She studied hard, then got to bed at a decent hour. I started adopting her schedule. Somehow my need for solitude and space didn't seem as important as the unexpected gifts of order and discipline.

We had been rooming together for four months when one night, as we were in our beds, Megan's voice came through the darkness, "Lisa? Thanks for letting me live here."

"Sure. You've been a great roommate." I meant it.

"I've never told you this, but . . ."

"But what?"

"The reason I moved out of my other dorm was because of a terrible roommate situation. A few weeks before Christmas I didn't think anyone cared about me. I was so despressed, I didn't want to live. That day I found you in the music room I was in really bad shape. Then you said I could move in with you—and that made all the difference."

I lay there marveling at the way God had brought us together, wondering which one of us had benefited more. Yes, I enjoyed a new friendship, clean room, and ordered living. But I had also discovered that when God was involved in my choices, I got something far better than what I had thought I wanted.

"I'm going to miss you next year," I said. "How about continuing on as my honorary little sister?" Even in the dark, I knew she was flashing a grin—one that had grown more appealing to me each day.

Alisa Bair

> I had also discovered that when God was involved in my choices, I got something far better than what I had thought I wanted.

© 1999 Randy Glasbergen.   www.glasbergen.com

GLASBERGEN

"We spend so much time together at the office, I guess the attraction was inevitable. But I never imagined I'd become obsessed like this. Now I lie awake all night thinking about that coffee machine."

....

Old friends are best—how old are you?

Ashleigh Brilliant

....

2

You Know Too Much!

As the saying goes, "You'll always be my best friend . . . you know too much!" That's why friends protect each other's secrets and dreams—to protect their own.

THERE'S SUCH A THING AS TOO MUCH ENCOURAGEMENT

Beth is not only a very good kidnapper, she makes a mean casserole to boot.

One day she dropped by to cheer me up. She brought with her this heavenly casserole. I mean, this casserole was amazing. It had tons of cheese and sliced eggplant and some eggs and tons of cream, and it had this Mediterranean-flavor thing happening, and it just melted in your mouth, and it was truly wonderful.

I get sort of passionate about food, if you hadn't noticed.

Anyway, so Beth shows up on my doorstep, and I make us some coffee, and we dig into her casserole, and we spend several hours just talking about life in general and my life in particular.

It was nothing short of a Kodak moment, all the encouraging and bonding and feasting that was occurring.

Early afternoon, I walked her to the door. She paused on my front porch, and our conversation began meandering toward good-byes. We chatted casually about nothing in particular, when suddenly I announced, "I'm going to make it."

Beth said, "I KNOW you're going to make it. You're strong. You're a wonderful person, and you've gone through some tough times but, yes, you're going to make it. And I'm going to be there with you every step of the way. No matter what the future holds, no matter what decisions you make with your life, I love you and I'll be there for you. You're going to be okay, Karen. This year is going to be a new chapter in your life. You're going to be fine. You really ARE going to make it."

By now there were tears in her eyes.

I blinked. I stared. Then I said, "I meant the casserole."

"The casserole?"

"I meant I'm going to make your casserole."

Karen Scalf Linamen

• •

Dave: I'll never forget the time we were ice skating on the lake. Suddenly the ice broke and I plunged into the water. You threw off your coat and shoes, and jumped in after me. What a pal.

Walter: What do you mean, pal? Why wouldn't I jump in after you? You had my jacket and skates on.

Bob Phillips

If you want to know how many friends you have, just buy a cottage on a lake.

Author Unknown

• •

WHAT A FRIEND

Throughout life, we'll have many different kinds of friends. Some will be "good time" friends. These are the ones who'll stay right by our side as long as we're having fun, but the minute things get a little tough, their loyalty fizzles. (Sort of like Peter's did the night before Jesus was crucified.)

Then there are the "what's in it for me" kind of friends. They're committed to the friendship as long as it's in their favor. Like an insurance company, when the benefits run out, they drop you.

How do you recognize true friends?

A true friend will find something positive to say about your new permanent, even though it looks like you bathed with the toaster.

A true friend is someone who puts a rubber snake in your sleeping bag at camp, then warns you about it.

A true friend can see you at your worst and not take pictures.

You can confide in a true friend . . . and rest assured that she won't confide your secret in six hundred of *her* closest friends.

A true friend will never walk out on you, even after you've shown her the door.

A true friend lets you vent, even though all that's coming out is hot air.

A true friend believes the best about you, even when everyone else is pointing to the worst.

A true friend knows you well enough to hug you when you yourself don't even realize you need it.

But for me, the real mark of a true friend is someone who, when I invite them over for a home-cooked meal, asks for seconds!

Martha Bolton

• •

A friend is someone who knows the song in your heart and can sing it back to you when you have forgotten the words.

Author Unknown

• •

KNOWING YOU, KNOWING ME

You understand what I have left unsaid. You appreciate in me things I have long since taken for granted. You suggest the improvements I need to make for areas of my life I had written off as hopeless. And you challenge me to use talents I deny or help me see when I'm chasing pipe dreams. You call me to higher aspirations than I can imagine for myself and give me courage to try new things. In knowing you, I no longer wonder who I really am because, through you, I see my own dignity, honor, and worth. Through you I am able to overcome my feelings of failure and weakness. In you I see a clearer image of me. In knowing you, I know me.

Mary Hollingsworth

· ·

If you're looking for a friend, I'd like to apply.

Ashleigh Brilliant

You can make more friends in two months by becoming interested in other people than you can in two years by trying to get other people interested in you.

Dale Carnegie

· ·

BEHOLD THE BIRDS

Gliding overhead they seemed almost magical to me—the birds of the air, as the Bible calls them. And often, at certain times in my life, they flew in to delight and comfort me when I needed them most. A little girl in West Virginia, I watched as the twittering wrens fluttered in their dust baths next to my grandmother's porch, and when the first robins arrived in the spring, I crumbled toast for them in the yard. Sprawled under our huge oak tree, I'd gaze upward hoping to glimpse a flash of scarlet—a cardinal—among the leaves. During our summer family gatherings Aunt Marcella and I flipped through her bird books, and one day we both let out a whoop when a rose-breasted grosbeak landed on the porch.

You'd think that when I moved to New York City I would have given up having birds in my life. Yet the terrace of my seventeenth-floor apartment was visited by warbling purple finches, cooing mourning doves, and an occasional raucous blue jay. Crows squawked on chimneys below, and seagulls sailed by from the Hudson River. City birds, you might say.

In 1988 friends and I bought a weekend house in the country. An amazing array of birds congregated at our feeders in the backyard. One incredible spring we looked out to see a gathering of goldfinches and indigo buntings, their colors bright as jewels.

It was the black-capped chickadees, though, that touched my heart the most, with their shining eyes, heads of soft black velvet and sweet natures. I'd go out to fill the bird feeder, and the chickadees would flutter down toward me calling "dee dee dee." I sometimes stayed there for a while, even in the freezing cold, as they came closer and closer, perching on branches barely inches from my head.

At *Guideposts* magazine, where I work, I'd often read stories from readers telling how God had sent birds to bring affirmation or peace or comfort just when they needed it. I'd hear from friends, who weren't particularly sentimental, about how birds had appeared at times of high emotion, cruising by to bless a wedding or christening, or tapping at the window of a grieving mother. Every so often it crossed my mind—as much as I loved birds, why hadn't I had such experiences?

When my friends and I decided to sell our country house in 1999, I knew I'd miss what I'd come to think of as my "country birds." One of our last evenings there, I went walking at twilight down a path through a cornfield close to the Delaware River. I paused at the top of an incline as the sea of leaves below me began to rustle, then churn. With a mighty beating of wings, perhaps a hundred swallows rose from the field and swept in unison into the sky.

A swirling, graceful ballet began that lasted for more than fifteen minutes. The swallows surged back and forth across the field, rising up, then skimming down, in elegant, pulsating waves. In the slanting golden light, the air seemed to vibrate along with my soul. Were these birds a congregation here for vespers? Finally, dusk settled, and so did the birds. The flock gave a final low turn, flew off across the river and was lost from sight. I took it as a beautiful benediction to my time spent in this country setting. Rather than regret at having to say good-bye to our house, I was filled with gratitude.

I'd read that 280 species of birds had been sighted over the years by devoted watchers peering through binoculars in Manhattan's Central Park. Back in the city, I kept hoping I'd see just one of my beloved country birds, but I never did.

And then came September 11. I stood numbly on my terrace that day. Above the drifting gulls I saw man-made birds on a darker mission—jet fighters patrolling the city sky.

In the weeks that followed, I felt a pervasive unease. I'd been thankful for my life of comfort—water pouring at the turn of a tap, fresh produce heaped in grocery stores, safe surroundings in which to work, opportunities to travel freely. Now my sense of security had been shaken. A dread undermined my joy in the city and the life I loved. I felt ashamed to ask God to help calm my anxiety—when so many others had lost loved ones, who was I to request any special comfort?

A month passed. Anthrax was found in Manhattan mailrooms, rumors of more danger circulated. As the weekend of October 13 approached, government officials announced the city was once again on "high alert" for possible terrorist attacks. Saturday morning dawned golden and mild enough for me to open one of my terrace doors. Still I felt almost physically sick with anxiety. I considered breaking a lunch date I had in the neighborhood with a business acquaintance. I could barely muster the energy to go out the door at all, much less carry on a conversation. I just wanted to huddle inside with my cats, Clarence and Sheila. What should I do?

Into my mind came a prayer I had taped close to my desk: "Open my heart to the gifts of this day." Inexplicably, I opened wide my arms and spoke out loud. "Holy Spirit, I need your help. Put me in touch with the strength and joy that remain at the center of each day, no matter how disturbingly the world has been shaken and changed."

There was a rush of air and a whoosh. Through my terrace door swooped a swallow, just like the ones I had seen in the cornfield that glorious twilight evening. The swallow shot across my living room, caromed off my ficus tree and dropped onto the rug. Clarence leaped from a chair, grabbed the swallow in his mouth and raced for the dining room, Sheila in hot pursuit.

"Clarence!" I shouted, fumbling to open some windows. In the next instant, just as astonishingly, Clarence opened his mouth and released the bird. For a moment all of us were still. Then the swallow spread its wings, rose from the floor in a graceful arc and swept out the narrow opening of the only window I'd managed to open. I watched as it sailed over the rooftops unhurt.

Within a half hour, I ventured out myself. I met my lunch date, blurted out what had happened, and we immediately started pouring out our hearts like old friends, sharing our fears about the future but laughing with the joyful surprises of life as well. When we parted, I impulsively turned down Amsterdam Avenue, a route I never take. Mid-block I paused at a florist shop and nursery. The sidewalk in front was filled with trees and hanging plants, a forest glade amid concrete and traffic.

I can't believe this is here, I thought. Then I heard a delightful "dee dee dee." It couldn't be. I gasped as a small bright-eyed bird with a dark velvet head fluttered down on one of the hanging baskets and hopped its way toward me. "A black-capped chickadee!" I cried.

"It's a sign, isn't it?" a lilting voice said. I turned. The woman beside me came up to my shoulder, had a gentle wrinkly face and curly white hair. Although she wore not a trace of other makeup, under each of her twinkling eyes was painted a line of lovely bluebird blue.

"You never see chickadees on the streets of New York City," I said.

"I know," she said. "It's a sign for you, from God." The chickadee gave a hop and flew up over a lamppost, toward Riverside Park. "Peace and blessings," the woman said. She walked around the corner and was gone.

"Do not be anxious about your life," Jesus said, "Look at the birds of the air: they neither sow nor reap . . . yet your Heavenly Father cares for them." And in a transcendent flutter of wings, in spite of the world's uncertainties, I knew that the timeless promise was true.

Mary Ann O'Roark

• •

Every man should keep a fair-sized cemetery in which to bury the faults of his friends.

Henry Ward Beecher

Treat your friends as you do your picture, and place them in their best light.

Jennie Jerome Churchill

• •

3

Lucy and Ethel Ride Again!

Every friendship has Lucy-and-Ethel moments, it seems—shared moments that collapse into hysteria and are forever enshrined in your friendship hall of fame.

TO LAMENT OR LAUGH

When my friend Charlotte moved into her new house, we spent several hours unpacking boxes and finally worked our way into the kitchen. She wanted to wash all the dishes before putting them away; so, we unpacked a couple of boxes and loaded the dishes into the dishwasher, only to discover that we couldn't find the automatic dishwashing detergent.

I said, "That's no problem; we'll just use this dishwashing liquid."

"Are you sure?" she said. "I thought you couldn't use regular liquid detergent in a dishwasher."

"Oh, not really," I said. "I've done it before, and it worked fine."

So, I filled up both detergent cups on the dishwasher door, closed the door and turned on the dishwasher. Then, we went back into the dining room to continue unpacking.

About ten minutes later, I walked past the kitchen door and glanced in. The entire kitchen floor was covered with soap suds, and they were getting deeper by the second. But I didn't panic.

I said, "You know, Char, you were right. You *can't* use liquid detergent in a dishwasher after all." *She* panicked!

The next hour was like a rerun of an *I Love Lucy* show. Every time I pushed the sponge mop into the soap suds, the whole sudsy floor moved away from me like a glacier. Charlotte finally held a wide-mouthed pan to the floor, and I chased the suds into the pan with the mop. She would pour them into the sink, rinse them down, and we'd start again.

We were winning the battle until we ventured to open the dishwasher door to face a solid wall of soap suds. We quickly slammed the door shut, trapping most of the suds inside. We decided the thing to do was to put the dishwasher on "Rinse" to wash away the suds.

Wrong! The hot water just multiplied the soap suds and sent them bubbling onto the kitchen floor again. And we were back to square one. Finally, using the sprayer hose on the sink, we were able to dissolve the suds with cold water. By then we were so tired from mopping and laughing we just went to bed. We decided that it was not the ideal method to employ but that she did, in fact, have the cleanest kitchen floor we'd ever seen.

It was one of those hallelujah serendipities that comes from a seeming disaster. It usually has to do with your attitude. You can lament or laugh. You can groan or giggle. You can snarl or smile. It's your choice. Either way, you end up

with a clean floor—the serendipity—and that should be good
for a small lip twitch or two.

Mary Hollingsworth

....

**It better befits a man to laugh at life than to
lament over it.**
Seneca

....

Fifteen Ways to Make a Friend!

Get a dog.

Exercise together.

Plan a neighborhood event.

Volunteer.

Attend a small group or women's Bible study.

Invite people to your home for dessert.

Consider attending a small fellowship rather than a
megachurch.

Assume the best about people you meet.

Be interested in the details of the lives of people around you.

Use memory tricks to remember the names of people you
meet.

Befriend the friendless.

Strengthen bonds with friends you already have.

Never, never, never entertain critical words or thoughts about your friends.

Be a good listener.

Don't panic during dormant times in your social life—use the time to rest, reflect, or regroup.

Karen Scalf Linamen

T AND D

In spite of her tiny size, she broke from her mother's womb fighting and fussing, and thankfully, perfect. Mona and Richard immediately named this long-awaited bundle of joy Tina, after Mona's mother who had recently passed away.

Naturally, it was no surprise that she was dubbed Tiny Tina almost from the start.

Mona and Richard delighted in their big-hearted and loving little girl. Her birth followed years of prayers for a baby, but they never dreamed they'd be blessed with such a beautiful and generous child. When Tina was five, Mona and Richard put practicality aside and bought her a purebred golden retriever. The puppy's golden coat exactly matched Tina's own blond locks, and they made quite the pair as they fast became best friends. She named the puppy Sandy.

It was hard for Tina to tear herself away from her buddy to start school that year, but resolutely she marched with her mom to the school bus to begin her school career.

That afternoon, when Mona met the bus, Tina came bounding down the steps, face aglow.

"Mom, I got a new name," she yelled. "The kids like me. They gave me a new name. The kids said Tiny Tina is too hard to say, and we already have another Tina in class, so guess what my new name is?" Tina spilled out her excitement in one breath. "My name is T. See, it stands for Tina. Isn't that cool?"

Breathing a sigh of relief, Mona told her child that T was a great name and, yes, she and Dad would also call her T. Mona was sure the nickname would fade away in the next few weeks.

The name stuck. By T's third year in school, no one but teachers even recalled her real name, Mona thought ruefully. T and Sandy remained inseparable when she was out of school. The dog accompanied her, whenever possible, on visits to friends, outings, and trips to the store.

It was for a simple errand to town that Richard decided to take along T and the pet. Mona blew kisses out the kitchen window at her little family, and they waved gaily as they drove away. On the drive into town, a truck hauling concrete blocks blew a tire and swerved head-on into Richard's lane.

There was nothing he could do, and he died instantly, the Highway Patrol officers assured Mona. They sadly informed her that the beautiful golden dog had been killed, too.

She slumped with relief, and with dread, when the troopers told her Tina had been badly injured and was on her way to the hospital. One of the men drove her car while she rode in the patrol car to the trauma unit.

For three hours Mona paced the surgery waiting room. Thankfully, friends had joined her by then and they murmured words of encouragement and offered prayers for Tina. At last a doctor approached the little group.

"I have very good news," he smiled at Mona. "Your daughter should totally recover, except for one problem. Tina's ears were badly damaged. She will probably never hear again. She is totally deaf."

Mona collapsed into her friends' arms. She tried to focus on the good news, but all she could think was her precious T would never hear her mother's voice again, and how could she explain her daddy's and Sandy's deaths?

Somehow, Mona made it through the next few days. With her friends' help she printed a letter to Tina about the car wreck. She could tell by Tina's expression that the eight-year-old comprehended that her faithful companion and her dad were dead. She didn't know if T's body-wracking sobs were for her loss or for the knowledge she'd never hear again.

When Tina finally arrived home from the hospital, she wandered the backyard morosely. She missed her doggy. At night she cried in loneliness when no warm, snuggly animal cuddled up next to her. When the doctors told Mona that she should try to enroll Tina in a school for the hearing impaired, Mona rebelled. She knew she could handle any needs of Tina's, and she was determined not to remove her from the only school and town T had ever known.

Within weeks, however, and despite going back to school, Mona recognized the signs of depression in Tina.

"It's because she can't communicate to her friends or teachers without a lot of trouble," the school counselor told Mona. "She really needs to learn to sign, and so do you."

"But she can still talk," Mona protested, panicking at the very thought of sending her little girl away to school.

"Yes," the counselor patiently replied. "But in a few years people won't understand her as she loses her ability to correctly sound out words. Mona knew the kind counselor was right, but she refused to entertain the idea of sending Tina away to school. She stubbornly researched for answers and finally found what she was looking for. A private academy for deaf children accepted day students who were not required to live on campus. The location was hundreds of miles from Mona's friends and relatives, but she resolved to make the move.

Mona thought her prayers were being answered when Tina seemed to regain her confidence at the new school. Unlike the first time, Mona was thrilled when her daughter came running in from school one day signing as fast as her little fingers would move.

"The school kids are calling me T, just like before," she spelled out. "Isn't that great? That means they like me."

"Wonderful," Mona signed back. She, along with other parents of hearing impaired children, had learned to sign quite skillfully.

But something still wasn't healed for Tina. Mona couldn't understand what was responsible for the emptiness she saw in T's eyes, the lonely look that would pass over her little face when she thought her mom wasn't watching.

The answer came suddenly one night when Mona glanced in the child's bedroom as she signed her nightly prayers.

"God, please send me another gold doggy," Tina prayed on her fingers, "one just exactly like my Sandy. Thank you."

She misses her dog, Mona thought. *I should have known that was the problem.*

Her thoughts were confirmed the very next day when Tina told her mom what she wanted for her approaching birthday which was coming up shortly.

"I want another golden retriever, Mommy," she said aloud. "Please, please Mama," the youngster pleaded.

Mona's heart broke, not just at the deterioration of Tina's speaking, but because her tight budget allowed no extra money for such an expensive purchase. "We'll see," Mona signed the standard adult answer for impossible requests from children. When Tina's face fell and her eyes filled with tears, Mona resolved that she would find a way to fill the void for Tina.

Every day when she arrived home from work, Mona scanned the classified ads. She called every dog breeder in the telephone directory, and there were golden retrievers, all right, to the tune of six hundred dollars a puppy. Inquiries at pet stores turned up similar reports. Attempts to persuade Tina to accept another, less-expensive breed of dog, were fruitless. Tears would flow, and Tina would tell her mother that God was surely sending her exactly what she wanted for her birthday—another Sandy.

The day before Tina's celebration found Mona on her knees. "Father, you gave us Tiny Tina, and you allowed her to survive the wreck, and I'm so thankful. Do you suppose you could shed your grace on her another time and help us find the perfect dog, one that I can afford? Do your perfect will in our lives, Father, I trust you."

After Tina left for school on her birthday morning, Mona received a call from a church friend. The friend had found a dog breeder who had a litter of golden retrievers ready to leave their mother. She had no idea of the price but thought Mona might be able to talk him into her price range, if she went to see him personally.

Hope filled her heart as Mona made the drive to the breeder. Sure enough, the puppies were darling and exactly the color of Tina's beloved Sandy. Mona's hopes were crushed, however, when the owner told her these pups were the same as the going price, six hundred dollars. Mona explained that it was her little girl's birthday and she wanted more than anything to replace the dog that had been killed in the car wreck along with her husband. The man was sympathetic, he told her, but he must make money on these dogs, because it was his living.

Turning quickly so he wouldn't see the tears which threatened to overwhelm her, Mona walked away sadly.

"Wait a minute," he called after her. When she turned back, he walked to the fence and picked up a puppy who had gotten separated from his littermates.

"Lady, this is a pedigreed puppy, but I'll never be able to register him, and none of my customers will want to buy him for show purposes." He cradled the little ball of gold in his arms. "If you want him, you can have him."

Mona couldn't believe her ears. There must be something terribly wrong with the puppy if the breeder couldn't find anyone who wanted him.

"What's wrong that no one wants him?" she finally dared to ask.

"He's deaf," said the breeder. "Born deaf. Do you still want him?"

"Oh yes!" Mona said through her laughter and tears. "I want him. In fact," she said, cuddling the golden puppy, "he couldn't be more perfect."

As she started toward her car with the wiggly furball, she stopped. "By the way," she asked, "does the puppy have a name?"

The man grinned. "Well, it probably sounds silly, but he loves to dig, so we just call him D.

Vicki P. Graham

"The medical profession is too obsessed with weight. Today my dentist said my teeth are getting too fat!"

A LOT LIKE ME

I like myself—I really do. Oh, it's not false pride as much as realizing that usually I'm all I've got. So, I'd rather be with someone I like for the rest of my life than with someone I don't.

Sure, I could be extremely hard on myself because I know my own faults better than anyone else. But the truth is, I'm doing the best I know how with all my heart, and I know it, whether anyone else can tell or not.

I love life and people and my work. And I've struggled hard through the years to be good at what I do. Oh, I know I haven't arrived yet, but I appreciate myself for who I am striving to become.

Sometimes I laugh with myself at myself, and sometimes we cry together. I have to take myself with a grain of salt (and a spoonful of sugar) and hope others will be gracious enough to take me that way, too. I give myself the benefit of the doubt and examine carefully my intent and effort, rather than my actual success or failure, for life is the striving, not just the accomplishment.

Yes, I like me—I admit it. I'm my own best friend. And because I like and accept myself for who and what I am, I can like and accept you as you are. Perhaps that's why I like you so much after all . . . you're a lot like me.

Mary Hollingsworth

MY BEST NEW FRIEND

I'd like to introduce you to my best new friend. I haven't known her very long, but it was love at first sight. She has huge, dark chocolate, brown eyes and hair to match. Her voice sounds like a young Demi Moore, husky and mesmerizing. She has the face of a cherub, with a gigantic dimple on each cheek. To put it bluntly, you just want to eat her up. She lightens up any room she enters and the space surrounding her becomes charged electrically. And trust me, you do know when she enters a room. My best new friend is four years old.

I really think she's part monkey. She scales the counters to reach high places. She pulls out drawers and uses them like a ladder. She dances on the table and sits on the windowsill. And she has climbed me from limb to limb.

You'd never know she was four by the lessons she's taught me. One time she was sitting across the table from me as we were drawing. I was really focused on my *Little House on the Prairie* masterpiece. Next thing I know, she has crawled under the table and is whispering in my ear, "Please put the colored pencils back in the box when you are finished, so others can use them." Ouch! I politely thanked her for reminding me to share. She didn't make a scene, just stated a simple request, then crawled back under the table to her chair. She glanced up, tossed me a killer smile, and went back to her artwork. Once again, I melted.

We've laughed, hugged, and kissed. We've talked in bed at night, showed each other our *owies,* rolled on the floor looking for tickle spots, and watched videos together. Things best friends might be inclined to do, well maybe nix the rolling on the floor part.

She's drawn me pictures, which I proudly display by my desk. Her snapshot, taken along with her sister, my other best new friend, is on my refrigerator next to the ninety-nine pictures of my son, Matt.

Our greatest creative achievement involved bowls of mint chocolate chip ice cream. It wasn't the green stuff, but the fake white kind. So we had to doctor it up with food coloring. I chose green of course, something about it being green just made it taste better! My best new friend went for the red. We stirred in the colors, playing all the while. Then I said, "Let's put blue in yours and make purple!"

Just as she dropped the color in, from across the kitchen came this voice, "Now only use one color." Oops! Caught by her mom! Quickly I told her we were having an art lesson in what two colors make purple. That was OK, as long as there was a point to the activity. These kids are home schooled, and everything in life is a lesson.

What I really learned from my best new friend was what unconditional love was all about.

What I really learned from my best new friend was what unconditional love was all about. On the day we met, she checked me out from a distance. A few hours later she was hanging on me like we were best buds. She brought out something in me I keep hidden just below the surface. She tapped into the child in me and set me free. I didn't have to act my age. I could act hers.

She cut and curled my hair in her home beauty salon at no charge; she owned the business. She fixed me tea in those cute little cups that hold about a dropper full. All she wanted to do was play with me. And I was more than willing.

Most importantly, she trusted me. She jumped from the rocks and the tree branches into my arms, never once thinking I wouldn't catch her. Her little hand would reach for mine as we walked the high desert trails.

I have found that age is irrelevant for having best friends. We can learn from each other and love each other, if only we are willing to open up and trust. If only we will share our life experiences with each other.

Whether you are four or eighty-four, you've something to share, something to offer, and something to learn.

Is there someone you know who needs a Lipton life? Time to get out the teacups?

Barbara A. Boswell

* * *

We cannot love anybody with whom we never laugh.

Agnes Repplier

* * *

SMILING

Smiling is infectious; you catch it like the flu,
When someone smiled at me today, I started smiling too.
I passed around the corner, and someone saw my grin—
When he smiled I realized I'd passed it on to him.

I thought about that smile, and then I realized its worth,
A single smile, just like mine, could travel round the earth.
So, if you feel a smile begin, don't leave it undetected—
Let's start an epidemic quick and get the world infected!

Author Unknown

THE GENTLE ART OF BEING THERE

Momma Millie is a chest thumper. The chest she thumps is her own. A most ample chest. It is a chest that, through all the expanding or shrinking variables of her more than ample girth, maintains a size or two larger than the rest of her, and holds within its folds a heart with a capacity for living and loving a size or two larger than the rest of us!

She makes of the thumping a personal vendetta, beating a slow staccato rhythm that rises in intensity until it becomes a heavy-handed thud, the pounding of her fist striking short, steady blows as though to beat up and out from the grass roots of her being all that is hidden within the nature of her human nature.

Her thumping culls the senses. Agony or ecstasy, delight or depression, outrage, anger, gratitude, joy . . . whatever the emotion, the thumping is the same. She tilts back her head and blinks her eyelids down, like two shades hastily drawn to shut out the blinding brightness of the moment, while strangled gasps of "Oh! Oh! Oh!" gurgle from her throat—an effervescent fizz bottled deep within the confines of her soul suddenly uncorked to the surface in popping, bubbly bursts, leaving her always breathless and, more often than not, completely discombobulated.

This is a vital essence of her charm—a willingness to be made vulnerable, to be set awry in the cause of caring and sharing another's life.

I first met Momma Millie, unwittingly, in the long corridor that was the maternity wing of St. Luke's Hospital in Pasadena. Our babies were born there two days apart, not only under the auspicious patronage of Luke, the healer, doctor-saint, but under the even more auspicious patronage of the sign of the cross. It was set up high, on the top of a glistening dome, etching a bright symbol of mercy and hope in the California sky.

"What sign were we born under?" my children would ask.

"Why, the sign of the cross," I would smugly say, "the best sign of all!" And I would slip it, like a talisman, into their young lives while my queasy heart whispered, "Keep them there, dear Lord, always under the mercy of your cross."

I met Momma Millie again, this time wittingly, at the annual bake sale of the Episcopal school, adjacent to the quaint cobblestone church that brings a whiff of English countryside into a corner of our small American town.

The rift of time of two days apart was soon bridged when her tot Tom and my little Anne were enrolled in kindergarten there. They were still auspiciously under the cross, but this time it was not on a rooftop but brought down to earth to swing on a cord around the necks of the teaching Sisters of Mary.

She was standing, like a majordomo, behind her own booth of home-baked goodies busily making change from a huge pocket in a floral wrap-around apron. Buns and breads and lemon squares were interspersed with jaunty little packets of homemade mints, pale pink and green, tied at the top with a bit of lace.

"My word!" I said, awed by the variety of her display. "Of all the things that you've got here, which would you recommend as best?"

"Apple-bar cake!" she said, with a snap of finality. "Baked it fresh at four this morning."

No dilly-dallying or coy shilly-shallying. I liked her matter-of-fact, direct response, but four in the morning!

I paid for the cake and asked her to set it aside so that I would not have to lug it from booth to booth. I returned some hours later to pick it up.

"Omigawd!" she gasped, as her lids blinked shut and the banging started, frantically and furiously against her chest. "I sold it again!"

"No matter!" I laughed. "Just bake me another and whenever it's ready, bring it up the hill and we'll both have a cozy cup of tea."

So, grown from the somewhat dubious seeds of two days apart and a twice-sold sale, there came into my life that joy of a friend to plant a memory garden in the soil of my soul and cultivate it through the many climates and seasons of my heart.

Momma Millie has the gift of *being there*.

The virtue of friendship is dependability.

Fay Angus

LAUGHTER AND GOOD TIMES

Regardless of culture or time or distance, we all bond together through laughter, dares, and crazy plans. Laughter is the evidence of the fun we are having in the moment, but it can also be a sign of healing and keeping our balance as life throws us curve balls. A hearty belly laugh, one that brings tears to our eyes and leaves us gasping, can make a lot of evils disappear. Whether enjoying the wit and silliness of our friends, shedding our good-girl personas (or watching others become bad girls on the big screen), or sharing a live radio show, laughter and good times cleanse away a lot of trouble and heartache and just generally sweetens our existence. We can always find these tools of enjoyment—laughter, making trouble, and other healing measure—with our friends.

Nance Guilmartin

• •

A man can always depend on three friends: an old wife, an old dog, and cash.

Henny Youngman

• •

"I've heard a lot about you—all nutty, of course."

OLD FRIENDS

When we moved to the farm, I discovered several columbines blooming in a weed-filled flower border. I was delighted. They were the same as the ones my mother had lovingly nurtured in the garden I knew as a child.

I weeded, fertilized and gave them loving care. One day an elderly neighbor told me that she, too, recalled this hard-to-find columbine hybrid in her *own* mother's garden.

I longed to give her some, but I had so few. I didn't want to risk losing them. Then, on impulse, I grabbed a spade and dug up the largest plant. After wrapping it carefully in damp newspapers, I handed it to her. "Here," I said, "I want you to enjoy them, too."

Several years later, during an especially bitter winter, my columbines died. When the snow melted, I watched in vain for the first green leaves and searched the border for seedlings. Nothing remained.

One May morning the telephone rang. It was my elderly friend. "I understand your columbines winter-killed," she said. "I planted mine by a south wall, and they're coming up beautifully. In fact I just discovered several dozen seedlings. I'll bring some over this afternoon."

So again I have my beloved columbines—because I shared with a friend.

"Give, and it shall be given you," the Bible says.

Yes, of course.

Grant me the wisdom to know that sharing doesn't mean losing.

Aletha J. Lindstrom

A FRIENDLY REMINDER

Friendships are a must for women. If it weren't for friends, women would have to go to the ladies' room alone. And who would offer a truthful assessment about whether an outfit makes your hips look big?

I have a Mustache Pact with my closest friends. If anyone of us goes into a coma, the others are honor bound by our pact to come and wax the mustache of the comatose friend. We women love to share those special moments.

I shared another special moment with friends recently. Several of us were hurrying to a surprise baby shower. We were hurrying because it's tough to surprise the guest of honor when she gets to the party before the guests.

We had pooled our resources to buy "the stroller to end all strollers." It was a collapsible stroller that would stroll the baby, carry the baby, swing the baby—maybe even change the baby—I'm not sure. It was Stroller-ama.

I told the others to run in while I got Super Stroller. I jerked it into position and started springing. Unfortunately, about mid-driveway, Stroller-zilla realized I hadn't fully locked it into place (emphasis on the aforementioned collapsible feature). It collapsed neatly into storage mode.

I probably don't need to give you a science lesson on "momentum," but let me mention I had a lot of it working for me. The fact the Stroller-nator stopped on a dime didn't mean much to my little springing body, which was immediately airborne.

Maybe you don't know me personally and think me ungraceful. Granted, you probably wouldn't want me to transport subatomic particles on a regular basis, but I don't want you to forever imagine me as a klutz. So maybe it would be better if you could please picture a graceful triple axel jump over the top of the stroller with sort of a one-point landing. I finished it off with a lovely flat-on-the-back pose, staring up at the sky for effect. I'd give it a 6.9.

Thankfully, I had my wonderful friends there to rush over and make sure I was okay. Of course, they couldn't actually ask me if I was all right since those dear friends were laughing so hard they were about to damage some internal organs! One of them couldn't even stay. She made a beeline for the house. You know what happens to laughing mothers.

That's another thing we love to share: laughter.

This is a little reminder. If it's been awhile since you've made time for friends, take the time and share a laugh with a sister. We need each other. There are certain things, concepts, even certain words, only women understand. "Mauve" and "taupe" are a couple of good examples.

Call up your special bud today. While you have her on the line, you might also want to take care of that coma/mustache thing.

Rhonda Rhea

•••

Last week a friend of mine lost his job at the orange juice factory. He couldn't concentrate.

Lowell D. Streiker

We were never strangers you and I—only friends yet unfound.

Author Unknown

•••

I ATE AT MY FRIEND'S HOUSE AND HIS FAMILY PICKED UP THEIR FOOD WITH SHARP METAL OBJECTS. I JUST COPIED WHAT THEY DID AND TRIED NOT TO LOOK FOOLISH!"

Together we stick; divided we're stuck.

Evon Hedley

4

Just between Friends

Friends share things that other relationships simply cannot share. Sometimes they're serious; sometimes they're downright silly. Whatever their nature, it's obvious that they happen just between friends.

FRIENDS OR SISTERS?

A good friend is my nearest relation.
Thomas Fuller

Charlotte and I have been best friends for more than twenty-one years now. It all started in 1985 when we met in the chorus at the big church where we both had just recently begun attending. And our connection was instant. In fact, the very first day, after I'd watched her interact with other chorus members, I said to her, "I'd like to get to know you better, because I think you're my kind of people."

She laughed and said, "Okay, want to go get a cup of coffee after church?" And we did.

Over coffee we found that we had very similar backgrounds and shared a lot of growing-up experiences. My dad was a preacher; her dad was a church elder. She's a teacher; I have a teaching degree. She's a gifted musician and I love to sing. We had both been married to ministers. Neither of us have children, except that she teaches them and I write for them. And the list went on and on.

We also found that we had some distinct differences. She's right-brained; I'm left-brained. She's a night owl; I'm a morning person. She's got a nose like a Beagle; I'm always lost. She loves sweets; I prefer salty snacks. And so on.

Before long, Charlotte, who has a masters degree in vocal music, had been asked to direct the chorus, and I, with my business degree, became the administrator for the group. And because it was a large and very active group that did outreach programs and concerts around the metroplex, throughout the state, and even overseas, we spent a lot of time together making plans, working out details, and the like.

Eventually, because we had become best friends and spent so much time running back and forth to each other's houses, we decided it would be fun to buy a house together. Of course, it took almost three years before we found a house that worked for two women with strong personalities who needed their own spaces. But we finally found one with two master suites—one upstairs and one down—that works perfectly. In fact, we've now been in that house for almost fifteen years, during which time we've remodeled it twice.

Over time, Charlotte and I have become more like sisters than friends. And evidently, it shows, because we are constantly being asked by strangers if we're sisters. (They say that dogs and their owners often begin to look like each other after they've been together for a few years. I wonder . . .) That always surprises us, because Charlotte has olive skin, brunette hair, and dark brown eyes from her partial Indian heritage. I'm a blonde-haired, fair-skinned, blue-eyed gal from German descent. We don't think we look anything alike, although we wear a lot of the same colors and styles.

Perhaps it's how comfortable we are around each other or how we tease each other and interact. We don't know, because it seems perfectly normal to us.

Once we were in London, England, shopping at Harrod's department store. On the way out of the store we stopped at their information desk to inquire about restaurants in the area. When the attendant finished giving us some recommendations, she said, "Are you two twins?" That was the kicker! We just died laughing and tried to explain that we were really just friends. She couldn't believe it.

Through the years, we've been asked if we're sisters so many times that we've just begun saying yes. It's such a hassle to try and explain the whole thing, and we've also noticed that people are a little disappointed when we say we're not. We are, after all, sisters in the Lord, sisters of the heart, and sisters by choice. And if that's not the definition of best friends, what is?

Mary Hollingsworth

• •

Friends come and friends go, but a true friend sticks by you like family.

Proverbs 18:24 MSG

• •

DON'T BE AFRAID TO BE FRIENDLY

My father was a bold and jolly man. He "never knew a stranger," as the saying goes. He used to embarrass my mother—in fact all of us—by his habit of addressing people he'd never seen before, on public conveyances, or at fairs and celebrations on the street.

"Nice day, isn't it? Say, this is some crowd." And he would introduce himself and pleasantly ask, "Where you from?"

"'Fools rush in where angels fear to tread.'" My mother would despair of him, shaking her head. But I think she envied and admired his lack of inhibition, for it freed him for rewards not enjoyed by more timid men.

For almost invariably the face would light up, information would be vouchsafed, often an interesting story volunteered. Sometimes for only a few casual moments, but often much longer, he would have made a friend.

> **"The way I figure it, life would be mighty lonely if there weren't some of us willing to break the ice now and then."**

"Everybody really likes to talk if he'd just admit it," Dad used to say. "Half the time people are dying for somebody to pay a little attention to them." He would smoke his cigar and chuckle, his bald head shining under the parlor light. "The way I figure it, life would be mighty lonely if there weren't some of us willing to break the ice now and then."

His philosophy makes more sense to me the longer I live. Propriety, good manners, good taste, the fear of being conspicuous, of being rejected, our motives misunderstood—such are the locks behind which too many of us quake, lonely, bored, and too shy to make the first move.

I once rode a hundred miles on a bus beside one of the most fascinating women I have ever met—before either of us had the courage to speak to each other and discover a common interest which kept us talking avidly during the scant half hour that was left. We all have been at cocktail parties where, overwhelmed by numbers, and failing to find a familiar face, we spend a miserable time—until somebody, some total stranger, takes pity on us and speaks. When, by the mere act of introducing ourselves, starting up a conversation, the evening might have been successfully launched. Not only for ourselves, but for someone else.

Don't be afraid to be friendly!

Marjorie Holmes

· ·

Friendship is one mind in two bodies.

Mencius

Two friends fishing on Sunday morning were feeling pretty guilty, especially since the fish didn't bite. One said to the other, "I guess I should have stayed home and gone to church."

To which the other angler replied lazily, "I couldn't have gone to church anyway . . . my wife's sick in bed."

Bob Phillips

· ·

FRIENDSHIP

And a youth said, Speak to us of Friendship.
And he answered, saying:
Your friend is your needs answered.
He is your field which you sow with love
  and reap with thanksgiving.
And he is your board and your fireside.
For you come to him with your hunger,
  and you seek him for peace.

When your friend speaks his mind
    you fear not the "nay" in your own mind,
    nor do you withhold the "ay."
And when he is silent
    your heart ceases not to listen to his heart;
For without words, in friendship,
    all thoughts, all desires, all expectations
    are born and shared, with joy that is unacclaimed.

When you part from your friend, you grieve not;
For that which you love most in him
    may be clearer in his absence, as the mountain to the
    climber is clearer from the plain.

And let there be no purpose in friendship
    save the deepening of the spirit.
For love that seeks aught
    but the disclosure of its own mystery
    is not love but a net cast forth:
    and only the unprofitable is caught.

And let your best be for your friend.
If he must know the ebb of your tide,
    let him know the flood also.
For what is your friend
    that you should seek him with hours to kill?
Seek him always with hours to live.
For it is his to fill your need
    but not your emptiness.

And in the sweetness of friendship let there be laughter,
and sharing of pleasures.
For in the dew of little things
    the heart finds its morning and is refreshed.

Kahlil Gibran

· ·

I have friends whom this world might call minimal
as far as not only their station in life, but their level
of intelligence and buying power. These friends to
me have been some of the greatest blessings that
I've known.

Fred Rogers

· ·

CLOSE TO HOME   JOHN M^cPHERSON

"Buying that mirror from that funhouse was
the smartest thing we ever did."

GRANDMA'S HANKIES

As a little girl, I would walk the three-block distance to the church from my grandma's house to attend Sunday school. Each week Mom and Grandma would take that time to visit, drink coffee, and solve all the family problems. Before I went out the door, Grandma would go into her bedroom and open her special box, take out a lacy hankie and tie coins into a corner for me to take for the offering. Some days the knot was tied so tight the teacher had to do the honor of untying it to free the quarters, dimes, or nickels.

I never thought much about dainty hankies until a special lady by the name of Carlene gifted me with one. While I thought it was so sweet of her, my first thought was, "Now what am I going to do with this?"

You see, I am into man-sized handkerchiefs. I mean, when I get a cold, I need something big. You know? The bigger it is, the more it holds. Ladylike just does not cut it.

My poor husband always knows when I'm getting sick, as his supply of snot rags, as I affectionately call them, disappear into purses, coat pockets, glove boxes, the cushions of the couch, under my pillow, and into the drawer next to our bed. It never embarrassed me to pull out the huge cloth in the middle of a meeting; it was simply functional. Honestly, I am so glad that men are becoming comfortable with who they are. These handkerchiefs used to come in only blue and red, with little paisley prints on them. Now they've given way to pink, green, light blue, and my favorite, neon yellow. Believe me, I've tried carrying the dainty ones, but it's either one blow and it's finished, or they end up in the bottom of my purse, and when the time comes to use them, they are coated in old dried-up chewing gum. And that is pretty rough on the nose. But I must admit, the wintergreen chunk that gets shoved up my nose does clean out the sinuses.

Over the years, I've seen pictures of crying women standing on the docks, waving their hankies to their men as they ship out to sea. I've seen Louis Armstrong wipe the sweat off of his brow after finishing up a rousing tune on his trumpet. I can remember both of my grandmas stuffing their hankies up their sleeves, or down into their bras for safekeeping. They always had one handy to wipe a runny nose. One hankie, three noses.

If the truth were told, you can usually find a roll of toilet paper in my purse to wipe a leaky nose. Hey, you tear off what you need, the roll gets smaller as you go, and you have sheets to share with a friend.

With this gift of a hanky, I found another use for it—to wipe away tears.

I don't know about you, but I think laughter and crying are so similar. Both use emotions, both create tears, and both make us feel better when we are done. And both are done better with a friend. I can go from laughter to tears and back again faster than a Porsche can go from zero to sixty. But it wasn't always true. It wasn't until God got hold of my heart and began breaking down the high walls I'd built, that there was even any need for a crying towel.

I pity someone who can't cry. With me, it's like the lava dome building within Mount St. Helens. It cannot be held in. The pressure is too great. When God melted my heart, He opened the tear ducts. What flowed in was compassion for His people.

When Grandma died, Grandpa asked all the grandchildren what we wanted as a remembrance of Grandma. One cousin took the china cups, one took the souvenir spoons. And, yes, you guessed it, I took the special box which held all of her hankies. What I didn't know was that I would find treasures hidden in the bottom of the six-sided box. Underneath the hankies was the something old I wore on my wedding day, a pair of pearl earrings.

Last year, I was taking a trip down hankie lane and dis-covered yet another treasure wrapped in a scarf. It was an odd-shaped ceramic dish, with the name of my grandma's good friend, Ione, scratched on the bottom. I bundled up the dish and walked across the street to my neighbor's house. You see, Ione was my neighbor's grandma, and she didn't have a single memento of her grandma's. Yes, the tears flowed. Yes, the hankies were pulled out.

Relationships with others are built by sharing, caring, praying, laughing, and yes, crying with them. Only when you give yourself away, do you truly find yourself.

Is there someone who needs to receive compassion from you? Stop being selfish. Give yourself away. You will be blessed seventy times seven more than the effort you put out.

Now, I need a hankie.

Barbara A. Boswell

●●●

Oh, the comfort—the inexpressible comfort of feeling safe with a person—having neither to weigh thoughts nor measure words, but pouring them all right out, just as they are, chaff and grain together; certain that a faithful hand will take and sift them, keep what is worth keeping, and then with the breath of kindness, blow the rest away.

Dinah Maria Mulock Craik

●●●

A FEW GOOD GUYS

A few years ago, I began to realize that many of those I con-sidered my best friends had moved far away, and if things were going to change, I would have to change them. So one morning I asked a new friend out for coffee and popped the question. "Hey," I said, past a mouthful of muffin, "how about we get some guys together a few times a month for a reading group? We'll discuss something serious, like Plato . . . or Archie. We can meet at my house."

The idea was met with a stifled yawn. "Phil," he said, "I'm busier than a wasp at a barbecue. Besides, a reading club sounds about as exciting as watching cheese mold."

"Well," I stammered, "how about we . . . uh . . . how about we get together and just eat. Ya, that's it. An eating club. We'll sample desserts, then have a lively discussion to burn off the calories."

"Now you're talking," said my new friend, squeezing the creamer way too hard. "Sorry about that . . . here's a napkin.

It's been four years since I cleaned that shirt. Four years since the Circle of Six began convening almost every other Tuesday. For reasons of international security, I can't say much, but I will tell you that each member has agreed to adhere to some strict guidelines as laid out in our red Principles and Procedures notebook:

Rule #1: Be there at 8:30 p.m. Unless you're late.

Rule #2: Hosts will be selected in alphabetical sequence. If you are hosting the event, bake something. We reserve the right to watch you eat it first. If you choke, lose consciousness, or die, we will try to revive you. We will not, however, eat your baking.

Rule #3: If you bring a cell phone, we will take it apart and hide the pieces.

Rule #4: No talking about Amway or Mannatech. Unless you have a really good story about someone who sells it.

Rule #5: The food must be better than last time we were at your house. If this means your wife bakes it, that's okay. No, your wife may not attend the meeting.

Rule #6: When we run out of food and things to say, the assembly is adjourned.

Tonight we're meeting by candlelight for my wife's cheese-cake. It is available in three flavors: Strawberry Slam, Triple Raspberry Rage, and Death by Chocolate. Helpings come in three sizes—the Ballerina, the Allegro, and the Cardiac Arrest. Collectively, we have gained more than 100 pounds in four years of Tuesdays. None of us quite knows why. We've also gained some friends. I wish you could meet these guys. A nicer bunch you're unlikely to find. A better-looking, wealthier bunch, perhaps. But these are the kind of friends you'd crawl through a minefield for. If I were heading into battle, well, I would take some Marines. But I'd want these guys to bring the cheesecake.

When I think of real guys, I think of Vance, Ron, Harold, James, and Glenn. And I think of the following characteristics:

Graceful. You should see these guys swoop down on a dessert. Such speed, grace, and elegance is seldom glimpsed outside ballet halls. But they are also full of grace when it comes to conversation. This is not Gossip 101. This is Sinners Anonymous. Overwhelmed by God's grace, we are looking for ways to pass it on. We do not spend our evenings pointing out the shortcomings of others, because we have encountered a few of our own. We also know that when you point a finger, four fingers are pointing toward you.

Understanding. Though we have come frighteningly close to tears on two occasions, if you come here looking for hugs and sensitivity, you may be disappointed. But if you're looking for some timely advice, or a listening ear, it's great to be sur-rounded by a few wise guys. In the Psalms, David prays often for understanding. In Psalm 119:34 he asks God, "Give me understanding, and I will keep your law and obey it with all my heart."

Yielded. We sometimes disagree on child rearing or music or automobile brands. But we share one thing in common. Each of us has handed the steering wheel over to God. Yes, we sometimes want to take it back or offer suggestions on how to drive. But we're learning. Together.

Successful. Tonight we got to talking about stuff we wish we had. About riding lawn mowers and power sprayers and hot tubs. Then we laughed. Though it's easy to forget, success is not defined by the stuff we grab, but by the footprints we leave. Our incomes don't define success. Our legacy does.

It was slow going at first. Guys aren't always comfortable talking about what's really happening in our lives. We hide behind the weather and the New York Yankees. But before long someone removes his catcher's mask and admits that he's just an old sinner in need of God's grace. And before you know it the clock strikes midnight and you're all sitting around wishing it hadn't.

Tonight we talk about a friend's failed marriage and what it takes to keep the flame burning. After we say goodnight, I sit on the sofa wishing that every guy on earth had this many friends. Guys who love to laugh. Guys who know that burdens are lighter and the path a whole lot brighter when traveled with a few fat friends.

Now, it's time to clean the candle wax off my wife's tablecloth. And, oh yes, I need to do something with this last piece of cheesecake.

Phil Callaway

· ·

Be slow in choosing a friend, slower in changing.

Benjamin Franklin

· ·

SOLITUDE

Solitude is creativity's dearest friend. She allows creativity total freedom to be whatever she must be. Creative ideas chase each other happily through solitude's park, playing hide and seek, each one secretly hoping to be caught and tamed. Other times, creativity curls up in the big, soft easy chair before the warm fire of solitude. And together they dream and doze and dream again. Solitude gently encourages her friend to give the most of herself, to be the best at what she attempts. And creativity responds with a sonnet, a symphony, a masterpiece, or a proverb. Rich friendship such as this is born of time—quiet, comfortable hours together dreaming and sharing.

Mary Hollingsworth

....

A friend is one who does not laugh when you are in a ridiculous position.
Sir Arthur Helps

....

THE PERFECT STRANGER

The rain poured down in sheets on the roof of the small house that my husband, John, and I had recently rented in Greece. It was midnight, and I was home alone with our fifteen-month-old daughter, Genny, who had been crying for the past two days with an ear infection. John was in the air force, gone to catch a plane to a German air base. I sat with Genny in my arms, rocking her gently, a warm bottle to her ear. Lord, please let the antibiotics bring Genny some relief.

A noise at the door startled me. "I'm so glad you're home,

John!" I cried. "Genny's not getting any better. She may have to go back to the doctor—" I then noticed that John wasn't alone.

"Hi, honey," John said. "This is James Walker." I looked at the black man behind John, all six feet and two hundred pounds of him. He was dirty and dripping wet, same as John. "Our plane's been delayed until tomorrow morning," John said.

"Hello, ma'am," Mr. Walker said, while taking off his jacket, trying hard not to drip water on the floor. "Sorry to impose." He looked at Genny, who was crying in my arms. The man began cooing at her, gave her a gentle tickle under her cheek. Genny stopped crying, seemingly transfixed by this stranger.

"Sweetheart, how about some coffee?" John said. I skulked off to the kitchen with Genny, who was crying again, and put her into her high chair. I got the coffee out of the cabinet. I'm sitting here with a sick baby, worried half to death—then he comes home with a disheveled stranger I'm supposed to make coffee for? I'll make coffee all right! I cleaned out the old coffee filter, and banged it against the garbage bin. John slowly entered the kitchen, shutting the door behind him.

"Let me explain—" he began.

"How could you?" I hissed. "It's the middle of the night, and Genny is sick. I've been up all night with her. I am not in any shape to entertain a stranger!"

"Please, let me finish," he said, holding me still for a moment. "I'm in line at the terminal behind James. He asks for a seat on the plane. The sergeant in charge is really rude to him, says, 'Sorry, buddy, retirees gotta wait till I deal with the important people.'"

"Big deal," I snapped.

"Just a second. James didn't even get mad. He tells the sergeant, 'I'm important in God's eyes,' then walks over to a chair and sits down to wait. When the flight was delayed till morning, the sergeant kicks James out of the airport."

"So?"

"So on my way home, I drove past a park bench. James was lying down on it, pulling newspapers over himself to keep warm and dry from the storm."

"Homeless? You brought a homeless man here, when I've got a sick child?"

"I just couldn't leave him there," John said sheepishly.

"What if he steals from us?"

John just looked at me, disappointed. He sighed and walked back to the living room. What could John have been thinking? Lord, please help me get this guy out of here as soon as possible. I picked up Genny and carried the coffee out to the living room, where John and Mr. Walker were engaged in conversation.

"I'm going to put Genny to bed," I said, before turning to look at John.

"Will you come back and join us?" the stranger said. "Please. Just for a few minutes." I said I would, grudgingly. When I came back, John poured me a cup of coffee.

"You look like you've had a rough night," Mr. Walker said.

"Yes, I have. So where are you going?" I asked.

"Wherever the Lord takes me."

I rolled my eyes. *Wherever you can find another easy mark like my husband to take you in,* I thought.

"I have something for you," the stranger said. He got up and pulled a soggy Bible out of his heavy coat. His fat fingers wrestled with the wet pages as he searched for the section he wanted. "Here's a piece of a verse just for you. Habakkuk, chapter two: 'Though it linger, wait for it; it will certainly come and will not delay.'"

"What does that mean?" I asked.

"Just trust in God," he responded.

That does it. I didn't need any Sunday school lesson from a homeless war vet. "I'm going to bed. Good night."

Mr. Walker stood up. "Thank you for your hospitality. This is much better than the park bench."

As I lay awake in bed, I heard the men talking long into the night. Please, God, keep us safe with that stranger in the house. And watch over Genny—I know that ear infection isn't going away.

In the morning, the men were gone. James Walker had left three addresses where he could be reached, not that I'd be writing. I put on some fresh coffee and got started cleaning the house—first straightening the couch that the stranger had slept on. Then it dawned on me that Genny wasn't crying. And she hadn't woken up during the night. I raced to her room to check on her. Genny was sitting in her crib, quietly playing with one of her stuffed animals. When she saw me, she squealed in delight, her ear infection apparently gone. It seemed like a small miracle. I didn't think she'd get better anytime soon. "Though it linger, wait for it; it will certainly come and not delay." A verse just for me . . .

I called John that night to tell him what had happened. Later we sent letters to each of the addresses that James Walker left trying to reach him. Each letter came back with the same response: Not at this address. John checked the base, and the military had no record of a retiree named James Walker.

I had complained about entertaining a stranger, and I wondered now why Mr. Walker hadn't pointed out that Bible verse about angels. For he was an answer to a prayer that I hadn't yet said. And proof that when you trust in God, he'll bring you a miracle. It may linger, but believe me, wait for it.

Norita Sieffert

THE TIES OF FELLOWSHIP

In 1765 John Fawcett was called to pastor a very small congregation at Wainsgate, England. He labored there diligently for seven years, but his salary was so meager that he and his wife could scarcely obtain the necessities of life. Though the people were poor, they compensated for this lack by their faithfulness and warm fellowship.

Then Dr. Fawcett received a call from a much larger church in London, and after lengthy consideration decided to accept the invitation. As his few possessions were being placed in a wagon for moving, many of his parishioners came to say good-bye. Once again they pleaded with him to reconsider.

Touched by this great outpouring of love, he and his wife began to weep. Finally Mrs. Fawcett exclaimed, "O John, I just can't bear this. They need us so badly here."

"God has spoken to my heart too!" he said. "Tell them to unload the wagon! We cannot break these wonderful ties of fellowship."

This experience inspired Fawcett to write a hymn. "Blest be the tie that binds our hearts in Christian love! The fellowship of kindred minds is like to that above."

H. G. Bosch

**"I can't get a good buzz going until
I've had at least three cups of coffee!"**

THE ARROW AND THE SONG

I shot an arrow into the air,
It fell to earth, I knew not where;
For so swiftly it flew, the sight
Could not follow it in its flight.

I breathed a song into the air,
It fell to earth, I knew not where;
For, who has sight so keen and strong
That it can follow the flight of song?

Long, long afterward, in an oak
I found the arrow, still unbroke;
And the song, from beginning to end,
I found again in the heart of a friend.

Henry Wadsworth Longfellow

UNSPOKEN WORDS

One evening, entertainer Mark Lowry called to tell me how much he appreciated me and my work. That night a friend of his, Rich Mullins, had been tragically killed in a traffic accident.

Rich's death came so suddenly that Mark regretted not having had more time to learn from him, talk with him, and share with him how much he admired his life and talent. So, Mark wasn't taking any more chances. He didn't want anyone else leaving this world without hearing the things he wanted to say. He was calling every friend and relative in his address book and telling them he loved them. It was already late in the evening, and he had just gotten to the Bs.

I admire Mark for taking the time to make those telephone

calls. How often do we think about telling our friends and families how much we love and appreciate them? And yet, we never seem to get around to doing it. Or we think we have to wait until we can do something big enough, meaningful enough, or memorable enough . . . then end up not doing anything at all.

When my father passed away, I was reminded how very short life is. So I made a vow that I was going to hug my mother and tell her how much I loved her every single time I saw her, which was almost daily. Most of the time she got several hugs in the same visit. Now that she's gone, I can't tell you how glad I am that I made that vow.

It's difficult losing those we love through death. And yet, if we tell them how we feel about them now, it will mean more to them—and to us—than all the tears we shed at their funeral.

Martha Bolton

● ●

True friendship is like sound health; the value of it is seldom known until it is lost.

Charles Caleb Colton

Friendship is the bridge between lonely and loved, between a glance and a gaze. It stretches from the fog into the sunshine, from hopelessness into faith. Friendship spans the gulf between despair and joy, between girl and boy. It crosses the chasm from hell to heaven, from God to man, and from you to me.

Mary Hollingsworth

● ●

··

The language of friendship is not words but meanings.

Henry David Thoreau

··

WHAT HAVE WE GOT TO LOSE?

I call it the year I impersonated an agent.

Not a secret agent, a la *Mission Impossible*. But a literary agent. (On second thought, it might have been closer to *Mission Impossible* than I realized at the time.)

It all began innocently enough. I was having my every-six-months lunch date at La Madeleine's with Tina Jacobsen. We always order the same thing: chicken caesar salad, tomato basil soup, strawberries romanoff, and lots of French coffee with good thick cream. We always talk about the same thing: How excited we both are about the forty-seven different new projects we've just taken on, and how crazy we are to have gotten ourselves so busy and exhausted from—you guessed it—tackling forty-seven new projects all at once. This conversation has changed very little in the last seven years, so we're thinking we must be gluttons for creativity overload.

Tina is one of those women who absolutely amazes me. She's so laid back and casual and comfortable to be around, a dark-haired Helen Hunt type with legs that wind around chair legs and crisscross on sofa cushions like limp fettuccini. She's as at home entertaining friends in sweats, surrounded by kids and boxes of cereal on a Saturday morning as she is in an all-business suit, negotiating with clients on Monday. Tina runs a terrific public relations firm, Books and Bookings Media, in a large (but still cozy) two-story-house-turned-office-building in the small town of Corsicana, Texas. Which is also famous for its fruitcakes. Not that this has anything to do with Tina, mind you.

Tina has several employees, a full-time on-site day care, and dozens of high-profile clients. I am constantly dropping my jaw at the things Tina will tackle with a "why not try it?" attitude. Just hanging around women like her fills my courage tank with confidence gas. (You know, I have a feeling my editor is going to make me change the metaphors in the previous sentence. But it's late and my creativity is lagging, so I'm going to leave it as is, and we'll see if I can get away with it.)

The first time I met Tina was by phone. She'd been hired to do the radio publicity for my first book. One hot summer afternoon she called and said, "Hi Becky, you ready for your first interview for *Worms in My* . . . ooops! My five-year-old daughter just tossed her shoe off her foot and hit herself in the head. Be back with you in a sec. . . ."

I knew from that first sentence out of Tina's mouth that we were going to be friends. She laughed when I later called to report on my first-ever phone radio interview. "Tina," I said, "I think I did pretty well in spite of the kids' letting Daisy and Colonel run barking through the house, and Gabe's holding up a rattlesnake he'd just killed in the middle of the interview. Thankfully, I was talking about being a mom in the country with critter-loving kids, so I think all the interruptions added a hint of authenticity."

Since that first encounter with Tina, there have been many more—mostly lunch—dates near Dallas malls, but we've also been on a couple of business trips together. And in spite of losing my purse in an airport bathroom on one such occasion, she's remained my very good friend. Today I do voice work for two of B & B Media's radio shows: *The Little Bookshop* and *Secret Place Devotions*. In exchange for my recordings, Tina helps advertise my Web site. It's the way women do business—we switch out, trade, help each other, and network in weblike fashion. (Men seem to prefer the less messy, but less fun, pyramid chain-of-command in business.) As Faith Popcorn, trend-predictor and business consultant, says in her newest book about marketing to women, "Women cross-pollinate. They take the powdery-fine residue from one story and dust it on the next. . . . Women naturally reinforce their bond by freely and clearly dispensing information, directions, or heart-felt helps."[1]

Tina's entrepreneurial savvy has always been an inspiration to me, and I suppose that's why that spring day at La Madeleine's, I nonchalantly answered, "Why not?" to her question, "How'd you like to be a literary agent and work under the umbrella of my company's name?"

After all, what did we have to lose?

How hard could it be to be a literary agent, anyway?

I had a bunch of friends back in Greenville and Dallas, and they all said they wanted to write a book. I'd been a first grade teacher and knew how to put together a portfolio for my class of students. I knew a few editors from my own publishing experience. Okay, so I knew *two* editors. Still, I was convinced that all I had to do was put two and two together and—*voila!*—out would come a bunch of published authors and we'd net 15 percent of their royalties.

So this is how I found myself three months later dressed in a bright blue power suit, pulling a suitcase full of my friends' manuscripts down the aisles of the Christian Booksellers Association Convention (CBA). Nobody told me what a naïve and gutsy thing it was for an author, new to this business herself, to call herself a literary agent. No one told me how ludicrous it was to try to sell manuscripts to senior editors at major publishers on behalf of friends, many of whom had never even published an article, much less a book.

And since nobody thought to tell me it couldn't be done, and Tina obviously believed in me, I just did it. Never asked another agent for advice. Never looked up *How to Be a Literary Agent* at the library. I just made a business card that said

"Becky Freeman, Literary Agent" and from there kind of guessed my way around the job and tried to think like an editor. And here's what I thought: If I were an editor, I would be tired of reading lots of little words on thick stacks of paper. All I'd want to see, at first glance, is a great title with a good visual hook, and maybe some pictures, photos, and cover art possibilities. I'd want the book summed up in one phrase, then one sentence, and if that intrigued me, I'd be willing to scan a paragraph. I'd want to read a one- or two-page easy-to-read outline with lots of white space and organized sections with headings in bold print. And I'd want to have an appointment set before the convention, where the agent made every minute count—pitching proposals in a short amount of time the way screenwriters pitch movie ideas to Hollywood producers.

So I visited with each of my wannabe authors/friends/clients and shared my vision. I honed down their proposals, helped them with titles, and asked them for something fun, colorful, and flat that I could use as a visual aid for their projects. If my clients' proposals got published, we'd have lots of wins to celebrate: They'd get advances and the honor of calling themselves authors, and I'd get to make a little profit from their success. But best of all, I'd get a whole collection of girlfriends with whom I could talk about writing. So, I made deep-breath phone calls and lined up a week of appointments at the convention with eight editors at eight different publishing houses.

When I saw two well-known agents walking down the hall at the convention, looking like Executive Ken dolls from *GQ Twins* magazine, for the first time since my enthusiastic start out of the agenting chute, I got nervous. I couldn't help notice that the sharply dressed duo each carried one neat leather briefcase. I was hauling around a small travel suitcase on wheels. One of my kids had wound an orange pipe cleaner around the handle in order to attach a couple of jingle bells to it. (Do not ask me why he did this. Does anyone know why children do half of the creative little things children do?) I could not, for the life of me, unwind the pipe cleaner, so I resigned myself to ding-a-linging with every click of my high-heeled shoes.

Peeking around a corner, straining for a glimpse of Real Agents at Work, I observed them opening up linen folders gold-embossed with their company logo and filled with professional proposals: thick slabs of pristine white paper covered with uniformly typed black words.

It was then that it dawned on me that there might actually be an established "system" for agents presenting proposals to editors.

I suddenly felt like Elly Mae Clampett, Literary Agent from Yahoo County. Or like little Loretta Lynn when she arrived on the doorstep of the Grand Ol' Opry from the hills of Kentucky with nothing but her geetar, a homemade dress, and a good-hearted man named Doo. (What I would have given for a good-hearted Doo right then who would hold my hand and assure me I wouldn't throw up when I sang my pitch and showed wares to the nice editor people.)

I sat down on a bench outside a convention door and unzipped my suitcase, which felt strangely like a hobo's knapsack at this point. I was afraid someone might offer me a sandwich or some change. Reaching inside the suitcase, I pulled out an enormous black vinyl binder filled with book proposals arranged Becky Style. In other words, my clients—these dear unsuspecting friends who had trusted me to represent their work—had given me their manuscripts, and I'd managed to arrange them exactly as one might expect an early childhood educator would.

Next to Ellie Kay's *Shop, Save, and Share* proposal, I had tucked in a picture of Ellie wearing a slightly askew crown and written underneath it: "Ellie Kay, The Coupon Queen." I'd also stapled one of Ellie's grocery receipts where she saved a

typical 60 percent on her week's worth of groceries and sur-
rounded that by stickers of bananas and apples and tiny grocery sacks.

Next to Brenda Waggoner's proposal for *The Velveteen
Woman*, I'd put stickers of soft, stuffed bunnies and then
stamped bunny footprints around her photo and professional
counselor business card.

Kali Schneider had found some beautiful stickers of chocolate truffles that I used to spruce up her *Truffles from Heaven*
manuscript.

Jane Jarrell, a Christian Martha Stewart (with a sense of
humor and a husband who likes her) gave me bright, colorful
proposals with cover sheets that looked like wrapped packages
along with magazine photos of her food-styling handiwork.

Annette Smith was a storyteller extraordinaire—the sort
that could make you laugh in one sentence and tear up in the
next, and so I had color highlighted the best paragraph in her
Whispers of Angels manuscript and dubbed her a "female
Robert Fulghum."

And on the list went. The more I stared at the hodge-podge
notebook of colorful pictures and photos, tucked between
short (albeit well-written) proposals, the more I wanted to run
out the door before somebody discovered I was an imposter
and arrested me before I could plead insanity.

But I'd gone too far to back out now. My friends were
counting on me. Tina had put her company's name behind
what I would represent. And an editor was calling my name.

"Becky, are you ready for our appointment?"

"No," I wanted to say. "But do you happen to have any
spare medication?"

Instead I put on my brightest smile to cover my deepest
fear—rejection—and walked into the publisher's booth, toting
my suitcase full of construction-paper-and-paste proposals
behind me.

Only God and His mercy and His great sense of humor could deliver me now.

Becky Freeman

••

Hold a true friend with both your hands.

Nigerian Proverb

••

1   Faith Popcorn. Used by permission.

5

That's Just What Friends Do

There's no explaining why friends do some of the things they do. They show up at just the right moment, say just the right thing, and always know how to lift your spirits or bolster your courage. Why? Because that's just what friends do.

Jack tossed the papers on my desk—his eyebrows knit into a straight line as he glared at me.

"What's wrong?" I asked.

He jabbed a finger at the proposal. "Next time you want to change anything, ask me first," he said, turning on his heels and leaving me stewing in anger.

How dare he treat me like that, I thought. I had changed one long sentence, and corrected grammar—something I thought I was paid to do.

It's not that I hadn't been warned. The other women, who

had served in my place before me, called him names I couldn't repeat. One co-worker took me aside the first day. "He's personally responsible for two different secretaries leaving the firm," she whispered.

As the weeks went by, I grew to despise Jack. It was against everything I believed in—turn the other cheek and love your enemies. But Jack quickly slapped a verbal insult on any cheek turned his way. I prayed about it, but to be honest, I wanted to put him in his place, not love him.

One day, another of his episodes left me in tears. I stormed into his office, prepared to lose my job if needed, but not before I let the man know how I felt. I opened the door and Jack glanced up.

"What?" he said abruptly.

Suddenly I knew what I had to do. After all, he deserved it.

I sat across from him. "Jack, the way you've been treating me is wrong. I've never had anyone speak to me that way. As a professional, it's wrong, and it's wrong for me to allow it to continue," I said.

Jack snickered nervously and leaned back in his chair. I closed my eyes briefly. *God help me,* I prayed.

"I want to make you a promise. I will be a friend," I said. "I will treat you as you deserve to be treated, with respect and kindness. You deserve that," I said. "Everybody does." I slipped out of the chair and closed the door behind me.

Jack avoided me the rest of the week. Proposals, specs, and letters appeared on my desk while I was at lunch, and the corrected versions were not seen again. I brought cookies to the office one day and left a batch on Jack's desk. Another day I left a note. "Hope your day is going great," it read.

Over the next few weeks, Jack reappeared. He was reserved, but there were no other episodes. Co-workers cornered me in the break room.

"Guess you got to Jack," they said. "You must have told him off good." I shook my head.

"Jack and I are becoming friends," I said in faith. I refused to talk about him. Every time I saw Jack in the hall, I smiled at him.

After all, that's what friends do.

One year after our "talk," I discovered I had breast cancer. I was thirty-two, the mother of three beautiful young children, and scared. The cancer had metastasized to my lymph nodes and the statistics were not great for long-term survival. After surgery, I visited with friends and loved ones who tried to find the right words to say. No one knew what to say. Many said the wrong things. Others wept, and I tried to encourage them. I clung to hope.

The last day of my hospital stay, the door darkened and Jack stood awkwardly on the threshold. I waved him in with a smile and he walked over to my bed and, without a word, placed a bundle beside me. Inside lay several bulbs.

"Tulips," he said.

I smiled, not understanding.

He cleared his throat. "If you plant them when you get home, they'll come up next spring." He shuffled his feet. "I just wanted you to know that I think you'll be there to see them when they come up."

Tears clouded my eyes and I reached out my hand.

"Thank you," I whispered.

Jack grasped my hand and gruffly replied, "You're welcome. You can't see it now, but next spring you'll see the colors I picked out for you." He turned and left without a word.

I have seen those red and white striped tulips push through the soil every spring for over ten years now. In fact, this September the doctor will declare me cured. I've seen my children graduate from high school and enter college.

In a moment when I prayed for just the right word, a man with very few words said all the right things.

After all, that's what friends do.

T. Suzanne Eller

••

The only way to have a friend is to be one.

Ralph Waldo Emerson

••

It Only Takes One

Ever wish you could do something to change the world, but get discouraged because there's only one of you?

Well, chances are you can't change the world all by yourself, at least not all at once. But you can change it . . . one act of kindness at a time.

Consider this—it only takes . . .

one compliment to make someone feel appreciated.

one visit or call to end someone's loneliness.

one show of trust to make someone feel trustworthy.

one offer of hope to end someone's hopelessness.

one request for help to make someone feel needed.

one person listening to make someone feel important.

one burst of laughter to make others want to join in.

one outstretched hand to pull someone to safety.

one person caring to make someone feel valuable.

one act of forgiveness to erase someone's guilt.

one hug to make someone feel huggable.

It only takes one person to change the world . . . one act of kindness at a time.

Martha Bolton

JUNIOR FRIENDS

I have learned to find fun in unlikely places. Fun is a mystery. You cannot trap it like an animal; you cannot catch it like the flu. But it comes without bidding, if you are looking for it.

Recently I made a trip by plane to Michigan for the funeral of a beloved aunt. As I boarded my return flight to California, I noticed a little girl, sitting all hunched up across the aisle from me. She looked so small and so afraid. The flight attendant told me she was traveling alone.

I thought, *Oh, well, the attendants will look after her.* I was busy going over the last few days . . . the funeral . . . the many people who had grown older since I had last seen them . . . It was all very depressing. I knew the five-hour flight home would be my only time to be alone with my loss. I had no intention of entertaining a little six-year-old who evidently had never been on a plane before.

As the plane took off, I noticed that she shut her eyes tightly and clenched the seat belt with bone-white knuckles. I felt something inside me want to ask her to come sit by me.

When we were safely in the air, I asked the attendant if it was all right, and she replied, "Oh yes! She has never flown before. Her parents have divorced, and she's on her way to California to live with relatives she's never even met before. Thank you for caring."

My "fun" started when the hostess came through with the complimentary beverages. Darling little Suzie with her dancing black eyes said she would have a 7-Up. I asked the hostess to put it in a fancy glass, with a cherry in it, because we were pretending we were special VIP ladies taking a super trip. Having 7-Up with a cherry in it in a fancy glass may not be your idea of fun, but to a six-year-old who had never had it that way before, it was great fun. We were off to a great start.

Our pretending went on, and I could see that I had missed so much in having all boys, never learning as a mother of a girl what little girls thought of. Suzie thought the luncheon on the plane was just like miniatureland. The tiny salt containers were a great joke. The tiny cup from the salad dressing was just for Munchkins. I had so much fun, enjoying with her child's eyes, all the goodies on our trays. We had our own special tea party. The little paper umbrella anchored in the dessert caused her to remark, "I got to see *Mary Poppins* once." I knew this was one of her most special experiences, and so we pretended that she was Mary Poppins. We kept her little umbrella, and Suzie had to learn to walk like Mary Poppins, with her toes sideways and holding the umbrella up just so. She did a great imitation!

Just taking Suzie to the little bathroom was an experience. She couldn't figure out how things worked. She wanted to know if the soap was small because somebody had used it almost all up!

When we returned to our seats, the attendant gave us both coloring books and three crayons—blue, red, and yellow. So together, we colored some puppies in the book red, made a yellow gypsy, and a blue ballerina. It was fun! She had lost her fear of flying, and we looked out on the cottony sea of clouds, talking about what fun it would be to walk on the clouds, holding our Mary Poppins umbrellas, and see how far we could go.

Then it was time to land. The hours had melted away. I had been a child for a few hours, playing her game, coloring her pictures, exploring her child's mind, seeing life through the eyes of a six-year-old. I had learned so much!

I will always remember that fun day, and when I eat on an airline flight, I always think of the "Munchkin" dinner Suzie and I shared that day. She got off ahead of me when we landed, and I rushed to try to catch up with her. I saw as she was swooped up into the arms of a grandmotherly lady with twinkles in her eyes. Suzie turned to me and said, "Look, Grandma, I am Mary Poppins!" She held her little umbrella up, turned her little feet sideways, and smiled a big smile of pure joy. The grandmother thanked me for looking after her, but *I* was the one who was taken care of that day!

It could have been a dreary, sad trip for me, lost in my own reverie of sorrow, but instead a little girl became a diamond of love and joy for me.

When life gets so heavy for you, and you wonder how you can cope with all the load, learn to put on the garment of joy for the spirit of heaviness, and fun is included in that garment of joy. Suzie turned my desert into a decorated place of joy. Look for that joy in your life, too. Don't settle for grouchiness and sorrow: settle for joy and happiness.

Barbara Johnson

. . . .

The better part of one's life consists of his friendships.
Abraham Lincoln

Nothing in this world appeases loneliness as does a flock of friends. You can select them at random, write to one, dine with one, visit one, or take your problems to one. There is always at least one who will understand, inspire, and give you the lift you need at the time. Fortify yourself with a flock of friends.
George Matthew Adams

. . . .

DURER'S PRAYING HANDS

From childhood Albrecht Durer wanted to paint. Finally, he left home to study with a great artist. He met a friend who also had this same desire and the two became roommates. Both being poor, they found it difficult to make a living and study at the same time. Albrecht's friend offered to work while Albrecht studied. Then when the paintings began to sell, he would have his chance. After much persuasion, Albrecht agreed and worked faithfully while his friend toiled long hours to make a living.

The day came when Albrecht sold a wood-carving and his friend went back to his paints, only to find that the hard work had stiffened and twisted his fingers and he could no longer paint with skill. When Albrecht learned what had happened to his friend, he was filled with great sorrow. One day returning home unexpectedly he heard the voice of his friend and saw the gnarled, toilworn hands folded in prayer before him.

"I can show the world my appreciation by painting his hands as I see them now, folded in prayer." It was this that that inspired Albrecht Durer when he realized that he could never give back to his friend the skill which had left his hands.

Durer's gratitude was captured in his inspired painting that has become world famous. And, we are blessed by both the beauty of the painting and the beautiful story of gratitude and brotherhood.

The Bible Friend

••

He is your friend who pushes you nearer to God.

Abraham Kuyper

••

• •

East Berlin was Communist controlled.

West Berlin was free.

Some people in East Berlin one day took a truck-load of garbage and dumped it on the West Berlin side.

The people of West Berlin could have done the same thing. But instead they took a truckload of canned goods, bread, and milk . . . and neatly stacked it on the East Berlin side.

On top of this stack they placed the sign: "EACH GIVES WHAT HE HAS."

Salem Kirban

• •

CONGENIALITY

The pleasure of your company is a many-sided affair. It includes the pleasure of seeing you, the pleasure of hearing you talk, the drama of watching your actions, your likes and dislikes and adventures; the pleasure of hunting you up in your haunts, and the delicate flattery I feel when you hunt me up in mine. I mean all this and more when I say that I find you congenial. Congeniality, when once established between two kindred spirits or in a group, is the most carefree of human relationships. It is effortless, like purring. It is a basic theme in friendship.

Frances Lester Warner (Adapted)

••

Love is rarer than genius itself. And friendship is rarer than love.

Charles Peguy

••

BROKEN HEARTS AND BURNT OFFERINGS

A package arrived. It wasn't my birthday, and I knew I hadn't ordered anything from a catalogue. Who was sending me something? Unwrapping the package, I found myself holding a most extraordinary heart, about the size of my palm. It was made of jagged pottery fragments—different-colored earthtone pieces mysteriously held together by an invisible force. The heart was a gift sent by a friend who sensed that in the aftermath of my divorce, this first Valentine's Day might be a reminder of unfinished dreams.

Sometimes we can go beyond a phone call or a visit to send someone something that speaks to us in its own way—whether it is a token to let a friend know you are thinking of him or her, something of yours that has special meaning, or an item that may, like this heart, symbolize more than your words could say. The gift took on even more meaning when I read the artist's story of how he makes the hearts. He makes these one-of-a-kind hearts by creating a beautiful pottery work, smashing it to bits, and then fitting the different-colored pieces together to make a new whole.

As the years passed, Valentine's Day became easier to bear, and yet this gift took on new meaning each time I faced a difficult situation. It was like a reservoir of care that I could return to when I needed a lift, some encouragement that what felt torn or rent would eventually mend. Gifts from the heart keep on giving long after someone's pain fades.

Nance Guilmartin

FULL CIRCLE

This is a story about me and a girl named Dorothy. We were in high school together in the little Upstate New York town of Wolcott. At the time we graduated in 1932 we didn't really know each other. But we were meant to be friends. All those years ago God could see my whole life from beginning to end, and I like to think my guardian angel set things in motion.

There wasn't much to do in Wolcott in those days. It was the Depression, and there were few jobs. People left for cities like Syracuse and Rochester. My boyfriend and I had plans to get married, but in the meantime I had an idea. "Sy," I told him, "I'm going to go back to school." The high school offered a six-month post-graduate term with all kinds of interesting courses. What's more, there was a new public bus service, and it ran right past my house. I could get to school as easy as pie!

And that's where Dorothy and I found each other. She took the bus, too, from her home in nearby South Butler. We shared an economics class, and got on right away.

From then on we chummed around. At noon hours, Dorothy would say, "Let's go shopping," and we'd head downtown. We couldn't afford to buy anything, but it was fun to window-shop and dream together. *What will our future be?* I wondered.

At the end of the school session, Dorothy had bittersweet news for me. "I found a job in Rochester," she said. I gave her a big hug, but I had a sense our young friendship wouldn't survive long distance.

Dorothy and I were both married the following year, and I guess our lives got too busy to stay in touch. We lost track of each other, but I never forgot my friend Dorothy. Sometimes I got out my high school yearbook just to look at the two of us.

For more than 30 years, Sy and I spent winters in Florida, going down after Christmas and staying till April. One of our two sons settled in New York, but the other moved to Florida. The Sunshine State kept calling me back too.

My health decreased as my age increased, and winters in New York were hard for me. So after I was alone in life, I bought a mobile home in Florida, near my son Paul. Still, I knew I would not be able to live on my own forever. My old body had been asking for help for a long time, but I couldn't find an assisted-living place that suited me.

One day a neighbor surprised me with a newspaper. "It's from Wolcott!" I said. "I can't believe it." She'd lived there too, and now subscribed to the hometown paper. From then on, I read the news when she was through. That's how I found my friend again—a photograph in the Wolcott paper. "It's Dorothy!" I exclaimed to my neighbor. "We used to be schoolmates."

She was celebrating her ninetieth year, just like me, and wonder of wonders, she now lived in Tarpon Springs, only miles from my son and me. The address of her assisted-living home was in the article. I wrote to her right away.

Dorothy wrote back immediately. "Come visit," she said. "What are you waiting for?" Seventy years had passed, but we were chatting like schoolgirls again. Only one thing had changed. "People call me Dot now," she said. I could get used to that.

How can I describe my joy at what happened? Paul and I made a date for lunch with her the very next week. There was Dorothy—I mean, Dot—looking lovely. This place really seemed to suit her.

"Can you believe us?" she asked. "We're ninety!" To me she was still as youthful as I remembered. We talked about old times and laughed so much we barely ate a bite of our lunch. Paul suggested that we look around, and take a tour of the home.

I made a down payment on a room there the next day. That, too, was meant to be. When I moved in a month later there were no vacancies.

More than a year has passed since then. Lunch and dinner with Dot are now everyday events. We play pinochle and bingo (she usually wins), and we go shopping in town, just like we used to do back in Wolcott.

"Remember so and so?" one of us will say. "Wonder whatever happened to her?" And then we get out our old high school yearbook and leaf through the pictures. Most of all, we talk about our miracle of being together again. We've come full circle, Dot and I, a perfect circle set in motion by an angel two lifetimes ago.

Marguerite Galloway

....

THE COMFORT OF FRIENDS

Someone told me that her favorite Scripture verse was, "And it came to pass." I looked at her rather quizzically, and then she laughed and added, "Just think. All this could have come to stay!" While we are in the passing-through stages, we have to derive comfort from others who have survived. Be a survivor, and help someone else!

Barbara Johnson

....

LISA, ARE YOU MY FRIEND?

I was fourteen and a pain in the neck, to be honest. I mean, I'd just run away from home; the best friend I'd ever had betrayed me in a way I never thought possible; my parents thought I was insane; and the only friends I had hung around me because, at the time, being a troublemaker's friend meant you were "cool."

The people I hung around ate up the stories I fed them of excitement and mischief. I suppose they respected me in some twisted way for having guts or something like that. But when I just wanted to be held or comforted, none of those "friends" were around.

The only person I felt deeply about, a boyfriend, I was no longer allowed to see. At first I prayed to God, "Please, please send me someone or something I can love again." Then after a while I stopped caring altogether. I had finally convinced myself and everyone around me that I had no need for anyone but myself.

I suppose that is when I became a real strain to deal with. And when my parents insisted that I had to spend the first two weeks of my summer working at a day camp for retarded kids, I acted mad. I wasn't really mad, just scared. Actually, I liked kids a lot. I told myself it could be worse. However, I didn't feel that way that very first day.

The volunteers and staff were required to ride the buses to keep order on the way to camp. I stepped up on the bus, smiled at the large black woman who was driving and reluctantly headed toward a seat. There were about five kids on the bus already. I tried not to look at any of them too long, smiling weakly and blindly at each as I passed. They grinned shyly back.

"Sit across from me!"

I turned my head to see a large black girl sitting in a seat, holding a tiny blond-headed boy. "Right here," she said, slapping the seat across the aisle while balancing the small child dangerously on her other knee.

Almost afraid to say no, I sat where she told me, and before I knew it she was unloading her burden on me. "You hold Robby now," she said. "You work here, not me."

Looking down, I found myself staring into the large,

vacant blue eyes of the little boy now in my lap. His mouth was open and wet, and his head bobbed up and down rhythmically as the bus bumped along the road.

"He can't talk," came the voice from across the aisle.

The black girl's eyes were still fixed on me. I was nervous but I tried to be kind.

"Oh," I said, "well, what's your name?"

"Karen," she beamed proudly. "I always hold Robby, but now you can. What's your name, girl?"

"Lisa."

"How old you, girl?"

"Fourteen."

"Ha!" she laughed loudly, pointing a kindly teasing finger at me. "You a baby. I'm seventeen!"

Seventeen! She acted like a three-year-old.

"Well, how old is Robby?"

"Six."

I was shocked. Robby was about the size of a two-year-old and he couldn't talk. He was a beautiful child, but he just kept babbling and rolling out sounds. His expression was blank; still, as the bus bounced and jolted along, he clung to me as if he knew I was there to protect him.

"You just wait till them crazies get on the bus," Karen was telling me. "Some of them really crazy." She tapped her temple with one finger, then moved it around in a circle.

I laughed. "Everybody's a little bit crazy."

"Hmph!" she said, throwing back her head. "You wait."

Robby was now standing and leaning toward the window. I slid over so he was right next to it. With his small hand he began spastically banging on the glass and calling, "Wawa." He was smiling. I looked out the window. We were crossing a bridge.

"Water," I said aloud. "I thought he couldn't talk," I told Karen.

She shrugged uncaringly. "He can a little."

"Robby, say 'Lisa,'" I said with slow deliberation. "Lisa." I pointed a finger to my chest. "Li-sa," I repeated.

For a moment he looked at me blankly as if I were an idiot. Then he stretched forth a hand and put it on my chest. "Nana," he said.

I nodded happily. "Yeah. Lisa."

"Nana," he repeated, nodding his doll-baby head.

Karen broke into a childish round of laughter. "He called you Momma!"

"Nana," I corrected her, rolling my eyes.

As the bus began to fill up I grew apprehensive. Strange faces loomed at me from almost every seat. A few other volunteers and staff boarded and smiled, but none I took a particular interest in. Mostly there were children. Some of them asked me over and over again who I was. Others just swung shy faces my way from the front of the bus. I felt like an exhibit. Even the staff seemed to be checking me out.

I didn't care what any of them thought. I was only doing this because I had to, not to please any of them or to hang around these kids for two weeks. Did they really think I cared?

A pair of green eyes winked at me from the seat in front of mine. I stared back. All I could see was a round shaved head and the squinty eyes that kept watching me.

"Hi," I said to do something to break the discomforting stare.

A round, cherublike face with buck teeth and no chin popped up quickly and grinned at me.

"Hi," said the little man. "I'm Brad. I'm gonna marry you."

"What?"

"I'm gonna marry you," he repeated, grinning slyly. "You gonna be my wife, you gonna be my wife," he began saying in a singsong change.

I rolled my eyes again. Oh, God, why have You put me here? All these people are going to do is make me crazier. Why am I here?

Brad followed me around the rest of the morning until the

campers were divided into groups by age. I breathed a sigh of relief when I found I'd be working with kids from eight to twelve years old; Brad was twenty-six. I thanked God.

By the end of that day, though, I'd acquired more "followers." There was Charles, the freckle-faced kiss-o-holic who grabbed me and planted one on me every chance he got, and Daniel, a skinny, grinning little black boy who sweetly slipped his hand around my waist and asked me to be his "best girl."

And there was Jeni.

Jeni was a chubby, thirteen-year-old girl with short, curly brown hair, a pug nose, and large, liquid-chocolate eyes. She followed me around, continuously asking questions:

"Lisa, what did you have for breakfast?"

"Cereal, Jeni."

"Lisa, what's your middle name?"

"Katherine . . . Now hang on, Jeni, I'm doing something."

"Okay . . . Lisa, what are you doing?"

"Jeni!"

Her questions drove me out of my mind. All the kids did. I didn't want them to follow me or hug me or hold my hand. How could they be so presumptuous to think I wanted their attention? How could they expect me to care about them? I didn't even know them. I didn't want to. I was afraid to.

That night, I told my mom I wasn't going back. Of course, she told me I had no choice. So I went to my room and pouted, and once again told God, "This isn't doing me any good, God. I need something more. I need a friend. These kids depend on me to take care of them, but God, I need someone to take care of me. Please help me."

No divine revelation came to me that night, so the next day I returned to camp, praying that the time might at least pass quickly.

On the bus, Robby was piled on my lap again, Brad sat beside me and Charles was waiting for me as I stepped off the bus. He placed a sloppy kiss on my mouth.

"Thanks a lot," I told him sarcastically.

He in turn flew into a hideous laughing fit and dashed madly across the playground to stalk another victim.

As soon as arts and crafts started, Jeni spotted me. I took a frustrated breath as she came and stood behind me.

"Hi, Lisa."

"Hi, Jeni," I tossed back at her half-heartedly.

"I missed you," she said.

I stopped what I was doing. Slowly I turned to Jeni, feeling an odd, almost warm sensation run through me. I faced her then. She was gazing at me with a tender, honest expression, waiting patiently for my answer.

"I—uh—thanks," I finally managed to spit out. I smiled at her with an unwanted feeling of gratitude. For what, I wasn't sure.

"Jeni," one of the staff members called, "come start your picture." Without another word to me, Jeni started off.

Before I even thought about what I was risking, I called, "Jeni, do you want to be my swimming buddy today?"

She turned, grinned a pleased, beautiful grin, nodded and then kept walking.

Suddenly, Charles's kisses weren't so bad, and Brad's proposals were actually kind of flattering. Every day on the bus, Robby would reach for me and call "Nana." I would look at the little doll of a boy and wonder, Why do you want me? What good am I? And why do I want you to need me? All of a sudden I found myself looking at those children in a new, glorious light.

I had learned something very special about those children. They didn't have any standards that they expected me to live up to. Whether or not I was kind to them, they would always be kind to me. Their love was pure and innocent and unconditional. I had been so wrong to think them foolish for being so open with me before they even knew me. That was their gift, their wonderful gift from God. I was amazed and touched by the love they gave me. They would have loved me whether or not I ever learned to love them back. Perhaps their possession of, and my lack of, that gift would have made me resentful and jealous at one time, but somewhere along the line, those children had sparked something in me.

For the first time in so long, I looked forward to getting up in the morning. I now had somewhere important to go and important people to see. I went to camp with growing warmth every day. The kids loved me, needed me. They wanted me there. If I quit, they would be disappointed. I knew how disappointment felt. It was dark and ugly and cold. They had saved me; the least I could do was not let them down. I now knew why I was here.

One day my group sat in a circle and sang along to a tape of the song "That's What Friends Are For." Jeni was at my side, and halfway through the song she began whispering questions.

"Lisa, have you heard this song before?"

"Yes."

"Do you think it's pretty?"

I dropped my arm around her shoulder, and we swayed back and forth to the music.

"Yes, Jeni, I think it's beautiful."

"Lisa, are you my friend?"

"Of course I am."

"Lisa, do you love me?"

I wiped away a tear that fell on my cheek.

"Yes, Jeni, I think I do."

Lisa Kerr

PORTRAIT OF A FRIEND

I can't give solutions to all of life's problems, doubts, or fears. But I can listen to you, and together we can seek answers.

I can't change your past with all its heartache and pain, nor the future with its untold stories. But I can be there now when you need me to care.

I can't keep your feet from stumbling. I can only offer my hand that you may grasp it and not fall.

Your joys, triumphs, successes, and happiness are not mine. Yet I can share in your laughter and joy.

Your decisions in life are not mine to make, nor to judge. I can only support you, encourage you, and help you when you ask.

I can't give you boundaries which I have determined for you. But I can give you the room to change, room to grow, room to be yourself.

I can't keep your heart from breaking and hurting. But I can cry with you and help you pick up the pieces and put them back in place.

I can't tell you who you are. I can only love you and be your friend.

Author Unknown

••

A man never likes you so well as when he leaves your company liking himself.

Author Unknown

••

FORGIVENESS

Forgiveness is not something we need, you and I, for I have accepted you as you are, and you me. You know that I am weak and make mistakes. I disappoint and hurt you, no doubt. But at the same instant you know it is without intention or malice. And I know the same of you. Because we have decided to be friends, we simply forgave each other once for all time—at the beginning.

Mary Hollingsworth

Simple vs. Real Friends

A simple friend has never seen you cry.

A real friend has shoulders soggy from your tears.

A simple friend doesn't know your parents' first names.

A real friend has your parents' phone numbers in her address book.

A simple friend brings a bottle of wine to your party.

A real friend comes early to help you cook and stays late to help you clean.

A simple friend hates it when you call after he had gone to bed.

A real friend asks you why you took so long to call.

A simple friend seeks to talk with you about your problems.

A real friend seeks to help you with your problems.

A simple friend wonders about your romantic history.

A real friend could blackmail you with it.

A simple friend, when visiting, acts like a guest.

A real friend opens your refrigerator and helps himself.

A simple friend thinks the friendship is over when you have an argument.

A real friend knows that it's not a friendship until after you've had a fight.

A simple friend expects you to always be there for her.

A real friend expects to always be there for you!

Author Unknown

Just as iron sharpens iron, friends sharpen the minds of each other.

Proverbs 27:17 CEV

6

The Best of Times, the Worst of Times

Friendship is a thick-and-thin kind of relationship. When things go wrong, your friend helps you cry. When things go right, your friend leads the cheer. And laughter is the element that keeps things in balance.

I'VE ONLY GOT EYELIDS FOR YOU

My good friends Linda Aleahmad, a licensed marriage and family therapist, and Mary Scott, a poet and administrative assistant to a Southern California newspaper editor, and I celebrate our birthdays together each year. We usually go out to a nice restaurant and talk about things like life, work, children, and of course, growing older. No matter how much we don't want to be reminded of it, the subject of aging almost always comes up, and we spend the rest of the evening comparing our latest physical changes and laughing about them as much as possible.

Tonight the physical change du jour was droopy eyelids. Each of us noted that our once perky eyelids had recently unperked themselves, and as Joshua might have said at the wall of Jericho, "They've come a tumbling down!" Not that we're tripping over them or anything, but they've drooped enough to give us that half-open, half-closed look that so many of us had through high school and college.

> **Tonight the physical change du jour was droopy eyelids.**

It seemed to happen to each of us overnight. Eyelids are sneaky that way. You go to bed with all your body parts exactly where they're supposed to be: Chin in place? *Check.* Lips in place? *Check.* Eyelids where they're supposed to be? *Check.* But when you wake up in the morning and look in the mirror, you notice that the rest of your body is exactly where it was eight hours ago, but your eyelids are now drooping like Deputy Dawg's, and you're just about as excited as he is about it.

I suppose we shouldn't be surprised. Our eyelids can't be expected to stay at attention forever. Forty or fifty years is long enough. They're pooped. They're ready for a break. They've faithfully served at their post and now they deserve a rest.

Unfortunately, though, their early retirement begins to place undo pressure on the eyelashes. They are the only things between the avalanche of flesh and our cheekbones.

A business associate of mine had her eyelids pulled back surgically. That's one solution, I suppose. And yes, it worked, but now she has that wide-awake look, like someone just said, "Boo!"

My friends and I spent the evening together weighing the pros and cons of getting our eyelids done but decided against it. We opted to keep the skin we're in and let nature take its course. We would be thankful for our health, our families, and all our blessings. It seemed like the right thing to do—

especially when we remembered that Thanksgiving was just around the corner.

I think there was something about my neck that reminded them.

Martha Bolton

....

A friend loves at all times.

Proverbs 17:17

....

KINDNESS IN A CUP OF COFFEE

Sharing.

Caring.

Loving.

Sacrificing.

These are actions of our friends and loved ones that have helped to lighten our load when the buzzards were dive-bombing the battlefields of our lives. So, we use those same actions to reach out to others. If we've borrowed a cup of sugar from someone in our time of need, then we ought to do more than ask for brownies. We ought to do some baking ourselves!

Several years ago while speaking on the same program with the late Dr. Charles Allen, I heard him tell a heart-warming story about Sam Rayburn, Speaker of the United States House of Representatives, who served in that position longer than any other man in our history. This story reveals the kind of man he was:

One night, the teenage daughter of a friend of Speaker Rayburn died suddenly. Early the next morning the grieving father heard a knock at his door. When he opened it, there was Speaker Rayburn.

Rayburn said, "I just came by to see what I could do to help."

The father replied, "I don't think there is anything you can do, Mr. Speaker. We are making all the arrangements."

"Well," Mr. Rayburn said, "have you had your coffee this morning?"

The man replied that the family had not taken time for breakfast. So Mr. Rayburn said that he could at least make coffee for them. While he was working in the kitchen, the father came in and said, "Mr. Speaker, I thought you were supposed to be having breakfast at the White House this morning."

"Well, I was," Mr. Rayburn said, "but I called the president and told him I had a friend who was in trouble, and I couldn't come."

Just think of those coffee cups filled with kindness. We've had more of them than we realize. Whether they were straight-up decaf or some Colombian mix, each had enough of a jolt to keep us going when the going was rough.

Flowers delivered to our house.

A pie.

An offer to baby-sit.

A phone call.

A greeting card.

Volunteering to mow our lawn.

A drive to the doctor's office.

Just random acts of kindness? Probably not. More likely, they were acts of care instituted by God and inspired in the heart of a friend. God will not fail us when the floods come. His mercy is everlasting—along with His everlasting friendship!

Stan Toler

Sooo ... these heels are too high, huh?

• •

A fair-weather friend is one who is always around when he needs you.

Great Thoughts

• •

FRIENDS OF THE HEART

I don't want to be just another friend that tugs away at you for your precious time, your attention, and your love. I want to be someone you come to for understanding, someone to whom you retreat for emotional rest. I want to be someone with whom you can laugh and share your joy, one on whose shoulder you can cry without embarrassment or apology and one whose hand you can reach for when you need comfort or support. I want you to be able to say to me, "I feel lonely today; stay with me a while longer." Or, "Can you come over? I need to talk to you." I just want to be there for you, as you so often are for me. I want us to be friends of the heart.

Mary Hollingsworth

ONE PERSON

Dr. Frank Mayfield was touring Tewksbury Institute when, on his way out, he accidentally collided with an elderly floor maid. To cover the awkward moment Dr. Mayfield started asking questions, "How long have you worked here?"

"I've worked here almost since the place opened," the maid replied.

"What can you tell me about the history of the place?" he asked.

"I don't think I can tell you anything, but I could show you something."

With that, she took his hand and led him down to the basement under the oldest section of the building. She pointed to one of what looked like small prison cells; their iron bars rusted with age, and said, "That's the cage where they used to keep Annie."

"Who's Annie?" the doctor asked.

"Annie was a young girl who was brought in here because she was wild. Nobody could do anything with her. She'd bite and scream and throw her food at people. I used to see her and think, 'I sure would hate to be locked up in a cage like that.' I wanted to help her, but I didn't have any idea what I could do."

"So one day I baked her some brownies and brought them in. I walked carefully to her cage and said, 'Annie I baked these brownies just for you. I'll put them right here on the floor and you can come and get them if you want.' Then I got out of there as fast as I could because I was afraid she might throw them at me."

"After that, she was just a little bit nicer to me. And sometimes I would talk to her. Once, I even got her laughing. The doctors asked me if I'd help with Annie when they examined her. That is how they discovered that Annie was almost blind.

"After about a year Annie went to the Perkins Institute for the Blind and later became a teacher. When she asked the director at Tewksbury if she could help in any way, he remembered a letter he had received. The writer was a man whose daughter was blind and very uncontrollable. He had written to ask if there was anyone who could help teach his daughter. And that is how Annie Sullivan became the lifelong companion of Helen Keller."

The doctor then remembered a statement that Helen Keller made when she received the Nobel Prize. She had been asked who had the greatest impact on her life. She said Annie Sullivan. But Annie said, "No Helen. The woman who had the greatest influence on both our lives was a floor maid at the Tewksbury Institute."

Rhonda Hogan, written with public facts

∙∙

It's the ones you can call up at 4:00 a.m. that really matter.

Marlene Dietrich

∙∙

UNFORGIVENESS

Dear Lord,
   I thought of Faye again today
   As I watched two little girls
   Walk to school arm-in-arm . . .
   Ours was a friendship of utter devotion:
   We traded prizes from Cracker Jacks
   We shared hair clips and diary secrets
   We whispered and giggled and wrote notes.
   Loyalty was our password.
   But one day the lanky boy in my life
   Discovered my friend was the prettier
   And our friendship was sadly disrupted.
   Lord, I can still recapture the hurt.
   I was miserable and mean.
   Words were harsh and unkind.
   She begged for forgiveness
   But I stubbornly refused:
   "Wait until after vacation—
   I might forgive you then . . ."
   But before our vacation had ended
   My friend and her family had moved—
   Leaving no forwarding address.
   Lord, even now I wish I could tell her
   Of the remorse I still feel
   And the wound in my life
   Because I refused to forgive.
   Wherever she is, does she know?
   I thought of her again today. . . .

Ruth Harms Calkin

The comfort of having a friend may be taken away, but not that of having had one.

Seneca

CLOSE AT LAST

Everything was ready for the luncheon I was giving: table set, chicken in the oven, broccoli steaming on the stove, sherbet glasses chilled. We were just waiting for the last guest to arrive. My future mother-in-law gave me an apologetic glance and said, "Sandy will be here any minute. She had another argument with her boyfriend and she wanted to patch things up."

"That's fine," I said. Sandy was my fiancé Brian's sister, and I'd been around the family long enough to know that she and her boyfriend had a troubled relationship. So what if she was a few minutes late? It would give the rest of us more time to chat. After all, this lunch was a chance for my mom and friends to get to know my future in-laws.

By the time we decided to eat without Sandy, the chicken was dry and the broccoli had turned to mush. When Sandy finally showed up I was fuming. How dare she ruin my party! How dare she let her problems spoil everyone else's fun! At least she could have offered an explanation, but, no, nothing. She sat sullenly at the table, stabbing a spoon at her melting sherbet.

Still, I kept trying with Sandy. When she got married—to a man who was not right for her—I gave her a pine chest with hand-painted flowers to match her bedroom set. Once, Brian and I took the two of them to dinner and the theater, but they arrived so late there was barely time to eat. She's family, I reminded myself.

But she wasn't a friend. We didn't have anything in common. At family gatherings we never had much to say to each other. After holiday meals she darted from the table so fast I assumed she preferred doing dishes to talking to me.

When my son's first birthday came, I went to the party-supply store that Sandy managed. "Why don't you make him a teddy bear cake?" she said. "I bet he'd love it!" It was the most enthusiasm she'd ever shown toward me. She filled my shopping cart with pastry bags, food dyes, colored sprinkles, and a special bear-shaped pan. I told her I didn't know a thing about decorating a cake. "Don't worry," she assured me; "I'll come over a couple hours early to help you."

But that morning, as I tried to decipher all the complicated instructions for the cake. I got a call from my mother-in-law. She happened to mention that Sandy was at the family's lake-side cabin, several hours away. She's supposed to be here! I wanted to scream. Why had I been foolish enough to depend on her?

After that I vowed never to count on Sandy for anything again. I could be polite; I could be cordial. I could even be generous, but that was it. I wasn't going to risk having Sandy let me down.

If she was coming over, I cooked dishes that wouldn't be ruined if she arrived late. For potluck dinners I asked her to bring salads or bread, things we could manage without if she didn't show up. Eventually she and her husband divorced. The family rallied around Sandy when she married again. As the years passed, I avoided her. I kept up a good façade when the holidays brought us together—one Christmas I went to enormous effort making her a calico goose after she had admired one at a craft show—but we were never close.

Then two years ago we went to the lake for Labor Day weekend. It was supposed to be a reunion for the whole clan, but at the last minute it turned out only Sandy's family and mine could make it. All I could think of was the strain of being in that cabin with the one person in the world I couldn't get along with. How would I keep up the polite chatter?

The first day we managed fine, unpacking, airing out the cabin, playing with the kids. We watched the children swim and cooked hot dogs and burgers on the grill. Exhausted and sunburned, the kids fell sound asleep after dinner. Our husbands were talking business, so I flipped on the TV. Just then, a bulletin flashed across the screen: Princess Diana gravely injured in a car accident.

Almost involuntarily I exclaimed, "No!" Sandy did too.

"It can't be . . ." she whispered, looking startled. "It seems like just yesterday I got up at five in the morning to watch her wedding."

"Me too," I said. "I always had this thing . . ."

"A fascination," Sandy finished my thought. We both had followed Princess Di's life, absorbing articles about her storybook marriage and its all-too-real dissolution. This latest news seemed like one more episode in a never-ending drama. I went to sleep expecting she would be all right.

The next morning before the kids were up I went into the

kitchen to find Sandy sitting with the newspaper. She glanced up, her eyes red, and handed me the paper. I stared at the headline in disbelief. Princess Diana was dead. My own emotions surprised me. I hadn't realized how deeply I sympathized with this beautiful, troubled woman. I wiped my eyes and looked up from the paper. My sister-in-law's gaze met mine.

"When Di's marriage fell apart," she said softly, "it reminded me a lot of my own. I'd felt trapped too. I thought I had to get married."

"What do you mean?" I asked.

"I thought that's what everyone wanted. Even though he was wrong for me . . ."

With that we began a conversation we should have begun sixteen years earlier. Sandy confided in me about the marriage that had gone wrong and the low self-esteem that made her think she didn't deserve any better. "I'm sorry for all those times I didn't show up when I said I was going to. I know it must have been frustrating for you. I was always so unhappy."

Here I had invested so much emotion in a princess I didn't even know. How quick I had been to forgive her failings! Why hadn't I been willing to do the same with my own sister-in-law? I felt like the man in the Bible who said, "Whereas I was blind, now I see." I had cloaked my relationship with Sandy in self-righteous civility, but I had never opened up to her. I might have given her things, but I hadn't given of myself.

Looking across the table, I thanked God for giving me a second chance—or maybe it was a fortieth or fiftieth. That was the dawn of my friendship with Sandy. A real, honest, straight-talking bond between two women who had more than family in common. We liked each other. We grew to love each other.

Today Sandy lives in a different state, but we're constantly in touch by phone and e-mail. We talk about our kids, the books we've read, what our husbands are doing and, yes, what's going on with the British royals. We plan our summers around the time our families can be together at the cabin by the lake. Again and again I'm reminded of how wrong I can be about a person and how right God can help make it. But the effort has to start with me.

Jane Kise

KEEP YOUR LIGHTS OFF!

Guess where I was last night . . . A Star Party! I know, it sounds glamorous, but it was a party celebrating the heavenly bodies in the sky, not the heavenly bodies in Hollywood. My friends have some fantastic telescopes that cost more than my car, and I thought it might be fun to learn about astronomy and meet some new people. Everyone brought their high-powered gadgets except me. I borrowed my nine-year-old son's Captain Hook telescope. (It's all I had!) Well, I met some folks who technically are classified as people, but they weren't like anyone I've ever met before.

I waited until dark and happily sped up the dirt driveway toward the telescopes. I jumped out of the car, skipped up to greet my new friends but had a hard time finding them because they were all in a giant cloud of dust I stirred up. I followed the coughing and choking sounds and joined the group. I was a little concerned at first because everyone was squinting like Clint Eastwood and they didn't seem very friendly. I pulled my girlfriend aside and asked why everyone was squinting at me.

She replied dryly, "You drove up with your brights on and we've been out here in the dark for hours. You blinded everyone. Next time, keep your lights off."

Well, I felt like a goober. Instantly, I went into my personal defense mode. *Drive with my lights off . . puh,* I muttered to myself. *So I blinded everyone. Better than running them over because I can't see them because my lights are off!* I felt better right away. I perked up and asked how they found their way around in the darkness.

"See the little red laser lights? Like that," she replied.

"Oh," I said.

And here I was copping an attitude thinking they all were superior to me with their laser pointers. I went back to feeling like a goober. Not to worry, though. I was sure I could redeem myself and win these people over once we went inside for tea.

We went inside for tea and everyone sat in a circle. It was like a human Stonehenge, very astronomical-ish. But the silence was deafening. No one was talking. Everyone just stared at each other. Deciding it was up to me to break the ice, I started chatting about newsy stuff. No one in the room read *People* magazine, so that idea went nowhere fast. I figured I had better relate to them on things they were interested in like computers and so on. I asked a few questions and received mono-syllabic answers. Finally, I could take the silence no more. I was going to liven up this place if it killed me; so I cleared my throat and defiantly announced, "I think the moon landing was staged!"

Girl, you have never experienced what I did at that moment. My ears popped because the room depressurized from the giant gasps of air being sucked into everyone's lungs. Time stood still. All eyes were on me and the human Stonehenge began to close up quickly. Soon, they were shoulder to shoulder, all holding their red laser pointers straight up into the air. It looked like a new millennium computer geek KKK mob scene. I smiled my toothiest smile and began reciting, "Though I walk thru the valley of the shadow of death . . ."

But then something wonderful happened! They were coming closer to me so they could explain everything there is to know about space, atmospheric pressure, NASA's budget, and on and on. They grinned at me and each other and at that moment everyone relaxed and began to enjoy the evening. Given time, I could envision a group hug. I learned a few things about astronomy. I cannot tell you much, because I don't think you would comprehend the enormity of the information I received. Okay, you're right: I didn't understand a single word anyone said, but I sure had fun hanging out with such brainiacs. You'll have to try it sometime. Just remember to drive slowly and keep your lights off!

Zarette Beard

● ●

Books are the quietest and most constant of friends; they are the most accessible and wisest of counselors, and the most patient of teachers.

Charles W. Eliot

Although the North American Indians had no written alphabet before they met the white man, their language was anything but primitive. The vocabulary of many Indian nations was as large as that of their French and English exploiters and often far more eloquent. Compare the coldness of "friend" with "one-who-carries-my-sorrows-on-his-back."

United Church Observer

● ●

LIVING IN THE MIDDLE OF A MIRACLE

I t was early in the morning as I drove toward Monty Bower's small, prefabricated office. I wanted to get there before developers and contractors and salesmen arrived. I needed a few minutes with my friend alone. When Monty saw my car he smiled, threw open the door to the office, and waved for me to come on in. That's just like him, I thought—always smiling, always opening doors, and always waving. He was one of the most winsome and optimistic persons I had ever known.

"Welcome to the jungle," he said with a smile, as he closed the door behind us. "If you're looking for a job, I'll put you to work today."

"No thanks, Monty. I've got more than I can handle trying to pastor a church. But if two or three deacons and a couple of old soreheads don't ease up, I may be back in a couple of days."

"Just let me know, and you're hired, Pastor," he joked with a big smile. "But let me warn you, the pay isn't all that great, and it won't be until I get this property developed. Heck, if I tithed my money these days, the church would be paying me!"

We both laughed, and then we were silent.

"How are you, friend?" I asked. "And what can I do to help?"

"I'm not really asking God for a big miracle," Monty said quietly. "I just need two years."

I listened without response. What can one say—even if he is a preacher—to a special friend who has just been told that he has six weeks to live?

"Two years is all I need," he repeated. "I'm not asking for a big miracle—just two years. In twenty-four months I'll be able to complete the development of this tract of land. I can build a new house for Jean and the children, and I can also oversee the construction of a house for you and your family."

"Monty," I protested, "you don't have enough time or energy to think about building me a house. We'd love to be in this new area of the city and in a house with more room, but that's not a priority with us."

"It is with me," he countered with a note of finality. I knew that when Monty talked this way, there was no room for argument.

"Now, put your current house on the market for sale, and tell Lawanna to go to work sketching off the kind of new house she wants. Bring that drawing to me, and we'll start ordering the materials. Tell her to get her plans completed soon, for prices are going up. Also, tell her she can change her mind as often as she desires until we start construction. After that, we make no changes.

"But Monty, I don't think you're in the condition to . . ."

"You leave that with me and the Lord," Monty interrupted. "You just make sure that Lawanna starts sketching some plans."

My friend knew what his goals were and he stated them firmly; but the smile across his face betrayed the sound of his voice. That smile, and the warmth behind it, made Monty everybody's friend.

I drove away from the temporary office on the site of Lochwood Meadows, a new development area near White Rock Lake, confused and bewildered. Lord, why? It doesn't make sense, I cried within.

And it didn't.

A few years before, one of Dallas's leading newspapers had carried a half-page story about Monty. He was a native of Dallas and a graduate of Southern Methodist University with a degree in business. Because of his reputation and integrity, he had been able to borrow one million dollars to buy one of the last wooded areas in Dallas for residential development.

This was a major undertaking for a thirty-five-year-old young man, especially in the middle of the decade of the sixties.

But challenges didn't bother Monty one bit; indeed, he thrived on them.

I knew this about my friend and was glad to see the series in the papers. But I also knew him as a devoted husband and father, a faithful churchman, and a sensitive, caring friend. Our wedding anniversaries fell on the same date, and Monty delighted in planning something extra special for the four of us to do in celebration of the occasion.

Then came reversals. First, there was the melanoma, followed by surgery. Then his younger brother who helped him in the development project was killed instantly in an automobile accident. About the same time, a financial recession hit Dallas and construction ground almost to a halt. Through it all Monty's optimism and faith did not waver. Nor did his goals.

Now, this new diagnosis: Both lungs were filled with nodules and fluid, and lymph glands saturated with cancerous cells. The prognosis: six weeks, at most.

Monty never slowed down. He was at work every day, pausing only to meet his surgeon in the emergency room of the hospital for the removal of another malignant node from his side.

"Look, Doc, I don't have time to lie up here in bed for two or three days while you take these things out. Just cut it out now, and let me get back to the office."

In spite of his commitment to fulfill his goals, there was nothing frantic or hectic about his lifestyle. He was busy, but there was a calm and quietness within. There was time for his wife, Jean, and their three young children. There was time for his parents and for friends. There was time for God and for worship. There was time to study Lawanna's sketches, coordinate the work of subcontractors, and oversee the building of our new house. There was even time to change the plans once after construction had begun. And he made the change with a smile.

"Monty," I said to him one day, "I'm concerned about you. You're pushing it too hard."

"I don't have time to die, Bruce. Not yet. I'm praying for time to finish these projects."

They were completed, all three of them. And more. Jean's house was built and the Lochwood Meadows development was saturated with construction. When we moved into our new home, one of the first things we did was to invite Monty and Jean over for a celebration dinner. Throughout the evening, Monty kept getting up and moving from room to room, grinning, and checking to make sure that every detail measured up to his standards.

Shortly afterward, his health began to fail rapidly. The last time I visited with him we talked briefly and had prayer together. I thanked him again for his friendship, and prepared to leave the room. He motioned me back.

Weakly, he signaled to me with raised fingers—two, then six.

Two . . . and six? What could he mean by that?

I moved back to the side of the bed, and he quietly said, "God is good. He always gives more than we ask. I asked for two years. He gave me two years . . . and six weeks."

And then he smiled.

Bruce McIver

. . . .

A true friend is the best possession.

Benjamin Franklin

. . . .

"MY MOM IS A LITTLE FREAKED ABOUT TURNING 40. TODAY SHE CAME HOME WITH A BOX OF PRESS-ON ZITS."

....

It's easy to make friends fast, but difficult to make fast friends.

Henny Youngman

....

MY OLD FRIEND

From the street it looked like an ordinary tree. It had green leaves, big branches and small flowers like other cherry trees, but my tree was different. It was a place for me to escape and let my imagination run free.

I was only four when my family moved into our house on Court Street, too young to know how to climb trees. Still, this one fascinated me. It was tall and majestic. It belonged to my neighbor, and I wanted it.

So I devised a plan to conquer the tempting tree. First mission:

make friends with the neighbor. Target: Frances Janeway. My strategy? Be a darling little four-year-old and win her heart. As it turned out, my plan worked so well that Fran Janeway became like a grandma to me.

My second mission: learn to climb the tree. On the side facing Fran's house was a cement core where part of the tree had rotted away. This I dubbed "The Step." It was the step between the real world and one of imagination and pure bliss. It was the step between a world of what I was expected to be and of what I wanted to be.

After many minor cuts and scrapes I climbed up The Step. Now there were multiple levels of the tree to explore. One by one I reached them until at last I had achieved my objective: the perfect spot.

My spot was made of three branches. One was covered with moss and the others were shiny and scrawny. It was like a throne. The large branch acted as the back and the smaller ones were the arms. From there I could see the whole world around me. It was like sitting on a cloud, floating above the earth.

In my tree I could be whatever I dreamed of being. I was a spy notorious for her cunning. I was an undercover agent with daring disguises. I was a soldier on a mission to save my sisters.

My tree was where I could sort through my troubles. It was a place where I could sit and think. It was my heaven, my sanctuary. I felt as if God were sitting on the branch next to me, taking in all my problems and bearing them as the tree bore my weight. There, I was surrounded by cherry blossoms like angels' wings, keeping me sheltered from the noise of daily life.

It reminded me of the story in the Bible when the Lord comes to Elijah. "The Lord said, 'Go out and stand on the mountain in the presence of the Lord, for the Lord is about to pass by.'" He wasn't in the wind, or in the earthquake, or in the fire. He was in a gentle whisper. I felt that whisper in the tree.

Then it happened. Mom and Dad said we were moving. My tree! I had to leave my tree and the memories that went down to its roots. The thought of leaving it made me feel sad and hollow inside, as if part of my heart were being torn away.

That was four years ago. This year we learned that Fran had cancer. The news wasn't good. Mom explained that if we didn't go say good-bye soon we might never get the chance.

We pulled into our old neighborhood and in front of our old green cottagelike house. I hopped out of our van and passed my tree without a glance. The blue paint on Fran's once well-maintained porch was all chipped. Even the small shrub under the gutter showed signs of neglect. Tears filled my eyes.

I saw Fran and the tears almost spilled over. Her skin was stretched taut and shiny over her bald head and emaciated frame. I feared I would crush her in my embrace. I had to work to put on a smile. Fran had always been so active and energetic. Now talking for just five minutes wore her out.

We said good-bye and headed out the door. I caught sight of the tree. The branches had overtaken the trunk so that The Step was barely visible. My memories of the tree came flooding back, only it was not me in the memories but my adopted grandma, Fran. I remembered helping her weed around the base of the massive trunk. I remembered my brother riding his bike for the first time without training wheels in Fran's yard and nearly running over her foot. I remembered being told to clean up the toys we scattered across her lawn.

I gazed up through the mass of branches and leaves and saw my spot. I knew then. I knew that even after Fran had gone home to the Lord and I had no reason to see the tree, I would still hold memories of my special friend and cherish the place that had brought me close to God.

Danielle Howden

....

Two are better than one; because they have a good reward for their labor. For if they fall, the one will lift up his fellow; but woe unto him that is alone when he falleth; for he hath not another to help him up.

Ecclesiastes 4:9–10

....

"MOM AND DAD, I APPRECIATE YOUR CONCERN AND RESPECT YOUR OPINIONS...BUT HOW CAN YOU SAY YOU DON'T LIKE THE FRIENDS I HANG OUT WITH?!"

....

A real friend is one who walks in when the rest of the world walks out.

Walter Winchell

....

FRIENDS TO THE FRIENDLESS

During the "Wake Up Crying" time in our family, when we had low dough, an unexpected baby on board, and a move to another state, I struggled to adjust to my new life. I gave myself a good talking-to. "Self," I said, "so you've had a run of tough luck. Enough! Get out and meet some people." So I signed up for a Bible study.

The first study was to be held in a home with brunch following. Sounded like a great idea to me—nothing like bolstering my faith and making new friends over chicken salad and bundt cake.

So on the morning of the Bible study, I slipped on my $19.99 red maternity jumper, told the roaches to stay off my counters, and drove off in my two-door coupe. After about twenty minutes, miniature mansions surrounded me. *This can't be right*, I thought. *Surely I've made a wrong turn.* But then I spotted a line of shiny SUVs parked in front of one mansion. A throng of Kathy Lee clones strolled to the entrance between matching topiaries. Feeling like I was about to go fishing for friends in a pond waaaay out of my league, I took a deep breath and mustered up the courage to go inside.

The teacher greeted me at the door and introduced me as a visitor. When the study was over and brunch began, the Kathy Lees metamorphosed into Chatty Kathies—to everybody but me. If I hadn't been hormonal and homesick for my familiar friends, I would have tried initiating small talk. Instead, feeling like a backward schoolgirl in a sea of socialites, I slipped out and drove home—wishing God had made windshield wipers for human eyes.

The following week, the study was, mercifully, held at the church. When I slipped in, the study had already begun, so I sat in the back row by two women I hadn't seen at the brunch. They welcomed me with kind eyes and warm smiles.

Soon, the duo began whispering wisecracks based on a humorous interpretation of the lesson—just loud enough for the three of us to hear. I gave into temptation and whispered a funny myself. They giggled softly, flashed those sweet smiles—and I was in like flint.

Nancy Wirth and Cheri Berry befriended this pregnant foreigner in a strange land. When I was embarrassed to invite them over to my apartment after the baby was born, Cheri sent me this e-mail about her own past housing woes:

> We had enough money to rent a quaint, three-bedroom Victorian. That was the end of the good news. It needed paint inside and out, and the walls were holey with termite damage. The neighbor to our left was an unhappy mother of three who eventually left her husband. She later told us, "When I compared my marriage to yours, I just had to leave." Great, so in addition to wreaking havoc in our own lives, we had managed to spread the wealth like a stomach virus through a preschool. The neighbors to our right had a Doberman that barked at the moon at the stroke of midnight.

After reading that, I complained about my apartment less. At least it was newly painted and termite free!

Rachel St. John-Gilbert

• •

Who finds a faithful friend, finds a treasure.

Jewish Saying

• •

7

Side by Side

*Companions. Sidekicks. Buddies. That's who
friends are. They come alongside us in life and
share the same events, emotions, and experiences we do. Side by side, no matter what.*

THE DUET

Vicki Graham and I have been best friends since we were
two years old—more than sixty years now (which neither
of us can imagine!). We grew up together in Sulphur,
Oklahoma, on the edge of Platt National Park. Our parents
were best friends at church, and we lived across the street from
each other.

Vicki and I were as different as night and day. I was a
princess; she was a cowgirl. I loved to stay inside and read; she
wanted to go outside and play. I liked to wear dresses; she
wore boots and jeans. But there were three things we both
liked: playing the piano, riding horses, and each other.

We took piano lessons from the same teacher for several
years when we were in grade school. And the teacher often

had us play duets for recitals and programs. We loved playing together, and it was something we continued to do for fun for many years.

Vicki stopped taking piano when she got out of grade school, but I continued taking all through high school and college, and eventually I became a music teacher, which I've now done for about forty years. Vicki went on to become editor of the local newspaper, mayor of Sulphur, a published author, and a licensed counselor. But back to my story.

We also both had our own horses when we were young, and we loved to ride. We rode in parades around the area and for local events. And we spent hours and hours out exploring the creeks and forests together on our four-legged friends. Sometimes we took a picnic and stayed out the entire day together (you could do that safely in those "good old days"). This, too, was a habit we continued for several years.

About 1958, when we were in high school, Vicki accidentally got her hand caught in her horse's bridle, and when the horse yanked hard on the bridle, it pulled off half of Vicki's index finger on her left hand, leaving her with one finger that was only half as long as the others. Fortunately, she recovered well from the accident—so well, in fact, that she often forgot about having a short finger at all.

One day in 1959 we were at Vicki's house just hanging out together, as high school girls do. And we decided to see if we could still play some of the old duets we had learned in grade school. We hadn't tried to play them in several years, and we thought it would be fun to try. So we sat down side by side on the piano bench as we had done so many times before.

I sat on the left, because I played the two-handed bass part of the duet. Vicki sat on the right, because she played the top two hands on this particular song. It was a fairly upbeat piece of music and Vicki's part had a dominant two-handed run of the scales in the middle of the song, while my part was the quieter rhythmic bottom notes.

When we came to Vicki's run, I was concentrating hard on my bass part when suddenly Vicki's part just stopped, and I glanced over to see what was wrong. Then I stopped short. No Vicki! She had fallen off the piano bench and was lying on her back on the floor with a stunned look on her face.

"What happened?" I gasped.

Then she started laughing. She laughed so hard she couldn't talk; so she simply held up her left hand to show me her half finger. She had been so engrossed in playing the duet that she had forgotten about her short finger. About halfway through the run of her scales, her short, left index finger missed the piano key, throwing her completely off balance and onto the floor.

We laughed so hard that we never did finish the song, and we still get a kick out of remembering our notorious nineteen-and-a-half-finger duet to this day.

We're best friends for life . . . and that's the long and the short of it!

Charlotte Greeson

• •

Don't walk in front of me, I may not follow.
Don't walk behind me, I may not lead.
Just walk beside me and be my friend.
Albert Camus

• •

THE TEACHER'S CHALLENGE

As a new teacher entering my sixth grade classroom, I was soon greeted by those teachers who had preceded me with those same students. They gave me a very vivid description of what lay ahead for me. For the past five years each in turn had tried every known method to deal with an incorrigible boy whom I shall call Will. To cope with his behavior, teachers had deprived him of playground privileges, paddled him, sent him to the office, and expelled him. Others tried granting him special privileges such as allowing him to be one of the captains when choosing players for the spelling match or the ball team—anything to build self-esteem. My friends warned me that all their efforts had been in vain.

By my third day I realized that my teacher friends had not exaggerated. In the classroom he repeatedly yelled out as I talked; he tripped anyone who walked down the aisle. Often he would lie on the floor or throw erasers across the room and even become profane at times.

I had no success in dealing with him in the presence of his peers; so ours turned out to be a "one-on-one" affair. In these sessions he was always in a sullen pout, sometimes refusing to answer me, other times yelling at me. Little by little I sensed a bit of devotion to his mother. Also I noted that he was very proud of his pet rooster, Sambo. When my patience was almost exhausted, I reasoned that we all have a weak, vulnerable spot somewhere. It was then that I resolved to find Will's Achilles heel. Finally I inquired if I might visit his mother and likewise get to see Sambo. His consent was slow in coming, but finally he did agree.

Before my visit I learned that his irresponsible father was a truck driver who seldom came home, and neither did his paycheck. The mother was terminally ill with tuberculosis and the fifteen-year-old daughter had dropped out of school to care for the mother.

When I arrived at Will's home, I found a very dilapidated house with meager furnishings. In the absence of chairs I even sat on an apple crate. The poor bedridden mother was very weak yet thanked me for coming. Next I got to see Sambo. Will had trained him to crow so that he might be rewarded with a few grains of corn. Also he would stand on tiptoe, then fly upward to get a morsel of bread that Will held high above his head.

Although Will was somewhat sociable when I visited his home, the old sullen, obstinate attitude was still very prevalent in the classroom. In privacy I often inquired about his mother or asked if Sambo had learned any more tricks.

My visits continued, and I took food and various articles to add to the mother's comfort. I even took seeds and a leg band for Sambo. I noticed a wee bit of improvement.

When school resumed following our Thanksgiving holidays, Will was at his worst, obnoxious to his classmates and completely ignoring me. At the close of that unbearable day when the children were going home, I plucked Will's sleeve and asked him to remain with me for a few minutes. Alone, I asked why he was so ugly today. I got no reply; instead he just stared, acting as if he could neither hear nor speak. Finally when I noticed that he was trembling, I laid my arm across his shoulders as he blurted out, "They killed Sambo so that we could have something to eat for Thanksgiving dinner."

The two of us sat on a bench side by side for a long time, my arm around his shoulders, with tears running down both our cheeks. Friends in loss. Friends at last.

India M. Allmon

• •

Meeting you was like suddenly seeing myself in a mirror.

Mary Hollingsworth

Panting and perspiring, two friends on a tandem bicycle at last got to the top of a steep hill.

"That was a stiff climb," said the first man.

"It certainly was," replied the second man. "And if I hadn't kept the brake on, we would have slid down backward."

Bob Phillips

....

....

H. K. Downie tells about a large newspaper that offered a substantial amount of cash for the best answer to the question, "What is the shortest way to London?" The entry which won the prize was: "The shortest way to London is good company!"

Henry C. Bosch

....

A FRIEND LIKE PATSY

My friend Patsy and I usually sat on either end of the pew, sandwiching our wiggly preschoolers between us. Today we sat side by side. It was my last Sunday in the church we both loved. At dawn tomorrow our family was moving to a farm near Copeland, Kansas.

I'd miss the church and our friendly Texas town. I'd miss living just down the road from my husband Don's parents. But most of all, I'd miss my friends. Especially Patsy.

Patsy shared all the bits and pieces of my life. Every Thursday evening she sat at my kitchen table and poked strained carrots down six-month-old Rebecca while I taught her oldest sons to play my battered upright piano. We shared recipes: my 50 hamburger dinners (we raised beef) and Patsy's zillion ways with zucchini (she loved to garden).

We helped with each other's moneymaking projects. Patsy's "earthworm experiment" went great until we had to sort 500 creepy night crawlers from tubs of manure. My cattle-checking venture was fun—until we saw a diamondback rattler on a day we'd worn shorts and sandals to hunt for baby calves.

We team-taught the junior-high Sunday-school class, provided oatmeal cookies for the Cherub Choir and took our kids for picnics when our husbands worked late.

What would I do without Patsy?

She read my mind. "You'll make new friends right away," she whispered, squeezing my hand.

"Not like you," I whispered back, choking down the lump in my throat. I already knew there wouldn't be any friends like Patsy in Kansas. Everyone said so.

The elderly couple from whom we'd be renting the farmland said so. "My dear," they told me, "prepare to be very lonely. There simply aren't any young people around here."

My mother said so: "Small towns aren't always friendly to strangers."

Don's mother said so: "It will be hard to meet anyone with you living eight miles out in the country. It's a good thing the children have each other for playmates."

The children had each other. Don had the farm. But what about me?

Patsy nudged my arm and we stood for the closing hymn, "What a Friend We Have in Jesus." I knew the Lord was my Friend . . . and the most wonderful Friend anyone could have. But I needed my earthly friends too!

Dear Lord, I prayed as the pastor gave the benediction, *please give me a friend just like Patsy.*

We set out for Kansas at seven o'clock on a chilly Monday morning in February. I drove our old white station wagon crammed with three children and a week's worth of clothing. A family friend loaded our furniture and appliances onto his truck, and also carried our German shepherds, Andi and Robert. Don's blue pickup brought up the rear. The back was piled with roped-down boxes of pots and pans, books and the baby bed. On the seat beside him Don had a basket of green-and-yellow tissue-paper flowers—the last project Patsy and I had done together.

We were a modern-day wagon train. I was certain we were heading into hostile territory.

We arrived at the farm too late to begin unloading, so we spent the night at a motel in a neighboring town. The next day, we got the kind of Kansas welcome I'd dreaded. While we ate breakfast, light snowflakes turned into a snowstorm by noon and into a raging blizzard by early evening. Andi and Robert, disoriented by the snow, ran away.

I'd never felt so alone! I sank down on a soggy carton, one that was dripping melting snow all over the kitchen, and started to cry.

Then the telephone rang. I was so startled I let it ring again and again. Who could it be? I'd thought the line was still unconnected, and no one even knew we were here.

Finally I picked up the receiver. "Hello?"

"Welcome!" a friendly voice said. "I'm Audrey Button. I live in the yellow house two miles straight east. The weather is getting nasty, so I thought you might want to know how to use the phone, because it's an eight-party line, and who to call if you need help."

She gave me a list of numbers, then we visited for several minutes. *Maybe this is the friend I prayed for,* I thought, *the one just like Patsy.* But no. Mrs. Button's girls were grown and gone, and she and her husband were semiretired. She was nice, but not at all like Patsy.

After two days of snow, the weather warmed up. I discovered there was something worse than being snowbound: We were now marooned by mud. Our two and a half miles of dirt road (heavy clay soil at that) dissolved into an impassable quagmire.

That's why we were surprised when, about nine o'clock one night, there was a knock at the door. "We're Howard and Ruth Stude," a pleasant, middle-aged couple introduced themselves. "We're your third-to-nearest neighbors." They apologized for coming so late and explained they'd been afraid to try our roads before they froze semisolid.

"We hope you'll come to our church," Ruth invited.

"We'll see," I hedged. The church she described sounded nice, but it couldn't possibly be like the one I'd left.

We went that Sunday anyway. The people were friendly and the building was lovely. There were two little girls Patrick's age and twins who were nearly four, like Michael. But no babies, and no one who looked like a replacement for Patsy.

That week I went to Copeland's one small grocery store. The aisles were very narrow, and Rebecca amused herself by grabbing things from one side while I was on the other—a box of oatmeal while I was searching for rice, a can of beans while I stocked up on corn. And she did it all from the seat of the shopping cart.

I was afraid I'd be banned. But Annie and Edith, the proprietors, just laughed. "We've been thinking of building a bigger grocery," Edith said. "If your baby is going to be a regular customer, we'll do it for sure!"

Annie made a sign about my dogs: Lost south of Copeland, two silver German shepherds. She posted it in the front window. (A week later the dogs were home, safe and sound.)

On my next visit to town I noticed a tiny building of corrugated tin right underneath the water tower. Copeland Public Library, a white sign read. Hours 2–5 Tuesday and Thursday.

Since it was 2:30 on Thursday, I went in. The librarian was a frail woman with sparkling blue eyes and hair as gray as the building.

"I'm new here," I told her. "Can I apply for a library card without having someone cosign it?" (My old library required two character references.)

"My dear, choose as many books as you like!" the librarian said. "Just sign your name on each card."

I chose three and took them to the desk. She stamped them, then indicated a chair next to her. "I'm Mrs. Ewing," she said. "If you have time, tell me about yourself."

We had a wonderful visit—the first of many. But much as I liked her, she wasn't the right age to be another Patsy.

Several weeks passed. My closest neighbor, Neva Patterson, held a get-acquainted coffee for Don and me. It was loads of fun, and I met many interesting people. But not one could replace Patsy.

When Patsy called to see how I was adjusting, I told her so. "I've met lots of lovely people," I said, "but they're all too old, or they don't have kids the ages of mine, or we aren't interested in the same things."

"So what?" Patsy replied. "You and I aren't the same age, and we didn't have much in common when we first met. You liked sports, I liked sewing. You read mysteries, I preferred romances. You liked comedies, I went for long, sad movies."

Funny, I'd forgotten all that. I'd forgotten that my friendship with Patsy had developed slowly and deepened over a period of years.

"You'll never have another friend like me," Patsy continued, "because I'm one of a kind. God only makes originals, you know. No carbon copies." No carbon copies!

No carbon copies!

In my search for a friend "just like Patsy," I'd overlooked the many "originals" God had sent my way. People like Mrs. Ewing, the store ladies, my wonderful neighbors. Friendship, I realized as Patsy and I said good-bye, wasn't a matter of age or family or common interests. It was sharing, and caring, and growing together. And it rarely came instantly.

God had been answering my prayers for a friend since our first day in Copeland. He'd brought a whole community of people into my life. In time, I'd have friendships just as beautiful and deep as the one Patsy and I shared.

Penny V. Schwab

....

Nobody, but nobody, can make it out here alone.

Maya Angelou

....

SHARING

Thank you, my friend, for your arm flung around my shoulder in a moment of comradery, for half your tuna sandwich when I didn't have time to make lunch and for the loan of your car when mine wouldn't run. Thanks for getting half wet so I could stay half dry under your umbrella. Thanks for holding my hand as we pray, for hugging me while we cry, and for laughing with me at the comedy of life. Thanks for the souvenir from your trip that means you thought of me while you were away. Thanks for sharing so much of yourself with me.

Mary Hollingsworth

••

A friend is a present you give yourself.

Robert Louis Stevenson

••

SISTERSHIP

Friendship is the ship the Lord often launches to keep my boat afloat. I seem to require people in my life. Scads of them. I am not the type who wants to be an island unto myself. (Unless it's Gilligan's Island.) Not that I don't want to be alone; my alone times are precious to me. I guard them and find solitude necessary for my sanity (well, what's left of it). Yet interacting with others encourages, nurtures, challenges, hones, and helps refine me. My journey has been made more joyous by connecting with friends.

One of my favorite dots in my network of friends is Carol. We are friends with history. We go back to the days when gumdrops were the latest rage in shoes. (Anyone remember those? They were a jazzed up version of saddle shoes.)

Carol and I still tell each other secrets and giggle over our silly flaws. We know the worst about each other and choose to believe the best. We have not always known how to do that. Then Jesus entered our lives and our friendship. He taught us important skills in esteeming one another. In our thirty-nine years of relationship, we have never not been friends; but since we met the Lord, our friendship has deepened in appreciation and affection.

We love to shop, decorate, antique, travel, dream, and scheme with each other. We have gone through the best of times in our families and the worst of times. We have celebrated and sorrowed together. We have guffawed and groaned. We have worshiped the Lord at the same church and studied the Scriptures in our homes. We have at times let the other one down, which gave us an opportunity to learn the imperative friendship skill of forgiveness.

Even though we share many interests, we are opposite personalities. I am boisterous; Carol is reticent. I'm a right-now person; she's an I-can-wait gal. Even physically we are opposites. She towers over my pudgy frame. Her hair is wispy and straight while mine is bushy and frizzy. Differences and similarities along with years of caring and sharing have enhanced our sistership.

Just three weeks ago I moved. I moved only seven blocks, but I still had to pick up everything and find a place to set it down in my new abode—that or have an enormous (thirty-four years' worth of stuff) yard sale. Thankfully, I had dear friends come to my rescue and help me pack.

After arriving in our new home, I was overwhelmed with the prospect of settling in. I had thought I would pull it together rapidly. Instead, I roamed from room to room trying to remember my name. Carol came to give support (and to verify my identity) every morning for four days. She assisted me until early evening, when she would then make our dinner, serve us, and clean up. You can only guess what a gift that was to me emotionally. I never expected that kind of beyond-the-call-of-duty effort, but I'm certain our new home ownership would have found me sinking before I could even unload the cargo, if it were not for Carol's life preserver of kindness.

What is it about moving that is so disassembling? The leaving of the old? The adjusting to the new? The disheveling of all our stuff? The initial sense of unconnectedness? Or all of the above? Carol's and my long-term connectedness served as a stabilizer during this turbulent time. And it was great to have someone with similar tastes to bounce ideas off of about furniture placement, window treatments, and picture arrangements.

By evening, when my wagon was draggin', Carol could catch her second wind and perform wonders in the kitchen. This girl can cook! Every night her feast renewed our strength and our determination to get back at it. The following day we would eat the leftovers for lunch, and in the evening she would prepare yet another culinary delight.

I'm thankful that the Lord knew we would need each other to survive various storms—and that he made available the harbor of friendship.

Patsy Clairmont

• •

When love and skill work together, you can expect a masterpiece.

John Ruskin

• •

SPECIAL FRIENDSHIP

Lord, this morning I thank You
With renewed appreciation
For the exquisite gift of friendship
And for my special friend
With her happy heart
Whose life is so intertwined with mine.

Thank You for her healthy optimism
Her enduring values
Her childlike trust in You.
Thank You for her creativity
So expansively shared.
Thank You for her direct honesty
Her radiant enthusiasm
Her refreshing freedom.
Thank You for her listening ear
Her ready response to needs.
Thank You for the way
Our thoughts walk arm-in-arm.
Thank You that together
We can be utterly ourselves
Without pretense—
Without fear.
Thank You that we can pray together
Laugh and cry together
Cushion defeats
And applaud victories together.
Thank You most of all, dear Lord,
That through the tested years
Our friendship proves to be
Another joyful way of knowing You.

Ruth Harms Calkin

MY TWO AMAZING LANDLADIES

My wife, Velma, and I had just returned from Sierra Leone, where we had served as missionaries, when my father suggested we see a place he hoped we could rent. It was half of a two-family home in Mount Vernon, N.Y., situated on a quiet cul-de-sac. The owners were a pair of elderly sisters, and it was their minister—an acquaintance of my mother's— who'd recommended us as tenants.

Velma and I were exhausted and our children were short on sleep, but, as the sun rose over New York City, we drove north from the airport to a quiet residential area in Westchester County and inspected the big, old house. The duplex for rent had three bedrooms, a separate dining room, and a spacious attic and basement for storage. *We'll never be able to afford it,* I thought.

Still, I contacted the agent. The price was way over our budget, but the agent was willing to have us meet the landladies. So on a brisk December day in 1982, Velma and I and our three children—aged five, three, and one—were warmly welcomed by the Delany sisters in their home.

I was charmed from the moment I met them. Intelligent, witty and fiercely independent, they are a link to another era. Born in North Carolina when Benjamin Harrison was president, they had migrated to New York during World War I, rubbing elbows with some of the best and brightest of the Harlem Renaissance. Miss Sadie Delany, the elder one, had taught in the New York City school system, and Dr. Bessie was one of the first black women to be a dentist in America.

It's probably just as well this doesn't work out, I thought to myself. After all, the sisters were well into their nineties. They couldn't possibly live in the house for too much longer. And would they really want our three rambunctious children right next door?

To our surprise, the day after our visit the agent called. The sisters would love to have us as tenants and were lowering the price. "It's an answer to prayer," Velma declared. I couldn't have agreed more.

So the Delany sisters became our neighbors, landladies, and friends. We tried to respect their privacy, but with only a wall separating us, we couldn't help becoming acquainted with their habits. The secret to their longevity was readily apparent. They ate healthily, exercised regularly, and spent a good portion of every morning in prayer. In the warmer months they could often be found outside, working in the garden. One day Velma looked out the window and was amazed to see Dr. Bessie, 92, climbing the pear tree, gathering fruit. "What in the world?" my wife gasped.

For a time we held a monthly Bible study in our home and the Delanys asked to be included. Their knowledge of Scripture was solid, but, more than that, they impressed me with their interest in the modern world. They wanted to know about my job at an alcohol rehabilitation center and Velma's teaching and the children's schooling. They talked politics. They kept an extensive list of concerns that they prayed through every morning, and it was an honor to know we were on that list.

And yet as up-to-date as they were, they resisted many modern conveniences—or inconveniences, as Miss Sadie might have said. They refused to have a telephone. When an emergency call had to be made, they used ours. The phone company pressed them to get a private line, but as Dr. Bessie explained to them, "Even if you gave it to us for free, you'd have to pay for someone to answer it, because we won't!"

Our children grew, but the sisters hardly aged. Once Miss Sadie told us about a memory test the doctor had given her. He showed her a few items and then put them into a bag, asking her which objects she remembered. She recalled every one. A year later, the doctor brought out the same bag. "Are you going to ask me what's in that bag again?" she wondered.

And she told him for a second time—a year later—every item that was in it!

I tried to help out when I could . . . replacing lightbulbs, moving furniture. When their TV broke down, I volunteered to get a new one. They insisted on a black-and-white. Do you know how hard it was to find a new black-and-white TV in the 1990s?

In 1991, just before Dr. Bessie turned 100, I decided to contact a couple of newspapers and convince them to do a story on the sisters.

The piece Amy Hill Hearth wrote in the *New York Times* brought them enormous attention. A publisher wanted them to do a book, and Amy worked with the ladies on that. *Having Our Say* became a bestseller. They were interviewed by TV's Charles Kuralt, and the night of the broadcast they came over to watch it on our color set. Dr. Bessie turned to me, shaking her head. "Look at what you got us into!"

With their unexpected fame we did all we could to protect the sisters' privacy. Meanwhile, they kept to their prayers, their churchgoing, and their healthy eating. Sadly, Dr. Bessie died in 1995, at age 104. Grieving, Miss Sadie slowly declined. She died this January, at age 109.

These days I run a homeless shelter in Westchester County. We get funding from many places, and recently we received a large donation from a charitable foundation. The source of the money? Royalties the Delany sisters earned from *Having Our Say*. And so they continue to help and inspire others.

Ron Mitchell

FRIENDTUITION

Even from across the room I can tell by the pitch of your voice whether you're happy or bored. And the slope of your shoulders says you're discouraged or exhilarated. Your hands let me know if you're nervous or calm. And I can see behind your eyes to your inner joy or pain. Your swinging foot says you are frustrated. And the way you play with your ring helps me guess your preoccupation. Some days you laugh and talk excitedly, but other days you're quiet, tired, and pensive.

The mystery of friendship is that two people, though separated by distance, can be so close. It's a kind of friendtuition, I believe. The sadness of it all is that two people might sit side by side and yet remain miles apart.

Mary Hollingsworth

8

Forever Friends

The joy of friendship is a forever kind of joy. Memories of happy, laughing times with our friends get pasted in our mental scrapbooks and stay with us always. Forever friends—the best friends.

FRIENDS TO THE END

It was Sunday after church, and three of my good friends and I decided to go out to lunch (our SOP). We chose an upscale restaurant in a nearby town that serves unusual, albeit pricey, Mexican food dishes—the staple of life.

As we were leaving the church building and heading out to the car, Charlotte said, "Can we stop by the grocery store so I can cash a check? I don't have any money." (This was pre-ATM, drive-through, grab-your-cash-and-run days.)

Since I'd been to the bank the day before and had plenty of cash, and in order to save time, I said, "Oh, don't worry about it; I have money. You can just pay me back later."

We got into my car and started toward Las Colinas—an expensive suburb of Dallas—where the restaurant was located. We were having a great time laughing and telling stories when about halfway there, Paula said, "Oh no! I just remembered that I spent my last twenty dollars at the drugstore on my way to church. I had to pick up some medicine for my daughter. I think I have about thirty cents left."

Again, knowing I had extra money, I said, "Well, no problem. I'm sure I have enough to cover the three of us. Don't worry about it."

"Well, if you're sure . . ."

"Really," I said, "it's no problem. Let's just go on and you can pay me back later."

We had a wonderful lunch together, enjoying the unique South-of-the-border cuisine and fun conversation. Being old friends, we had a lot of shared experiences that we delighted in reliving over hot sauce and blue tortilla chips. We even shared a couple of high-class desserts to top the meal off on a sweet note. As we were finishing our coffee, the waiter brought the bill.

Sher picked up the bill, looked at the total, and reached for her purse. She pulled out her wallet, looked inside, and then turned an embarrassed scarlet. "Well, you're never gonna believe hits," she whispered, "but I don't have any money either."

"You're kidding, right?" I asked hopefully.

"No," she said beginning to giggle nervously. "I'm as serious as a heart attack. I have *no* money. I forgot to go to the bank yesterday."

"Oh, wonderful!" I said. "Well, it's nice to have such a great bunch of moochers for friends," I said teasingly.

Everyone broke out laughing. The people sitting around us looked over to see what was so funny. At the same time, my three true and faithful friends all turned and looked at me with expectant expressions. Fortunately, being the only left-brained one in the bunch, I tended to plan ahead and follow my old Girl Scout motto: "Be prepared." But even I was a little worried about whether I could cover the entire bill with the money I had.

I held out my hand and Sher gave me the bill. I knew I had exactly $80.00 in my purse. When I turned the bill over, it was $72.98. With a 10 percent tip for our waiter, the total was $80.28.

I put the $80 in the folder with the bill. And Paula said, "Wait!" She took out her purse and handed me the thirty cents she had left, which put us over the top by two whole pennies. When the waiter came to take the payment, I handed him the folder.

He said, "I'll be right back with your change, ladies."

And I said, "No, please just keep the change."

At that moment, my friends and I burst out laughing, grabbed our purses, and sprinted for the door. In our wake were about twenty tables of dignified restaurant guests with shocked looks on their faces, wondering what could possibly be so funny about paying the bill in such a pricey establishment.

We, however, laughed all the way home, and even today— more than fifteen years later—my three favorite moochers and I get a great laugh out of reliving that adventure. And before we go out to eat these days, I always ask, "Does everybody . . . or anybody . . . have money?"

We celebrate being friends to the end . . . of the money!

Mary Hollingsworth

· ·

She's my best friend. She thinks I'm too thin, and I think she's a natural blond.
Carrie Snow

· ·

••

And the song, from beginning to end, I found in the heart of a friend.

Henry Wadsworth Longfellow

••

FOREVER FRIENDS

A best friend can last your whole life, so when you're old you'll have someone who shares your memories and knew you "when"—then the laughter never has to end. They're easiest to come by when you're young, so if you're ten and reading this, get all the best friends you can and never lose them. Here are some ideas on where to find new friends: Get involved with something that meets regularly and for a long time, so friendship has a chance to develop. Join a book club, or an investment club, sewing or craft classes, creative writing classes, a meditation group, yoga class, or exercise group. You can volunteer to support a candidate, be a Big Sister, put together a fund raiser, be a Girl Scout leader, or join the Junior League. To keep a best friend you have to be nice, be loyal, and be forgiving. To have a best friend you must BE a best friend. To be loved, you must be loveable. The rewards? Support, solace, fun, encouragement, comfort, trust, adventure, love, and laughter.

Susan Branch

••

Yes'm, old friends is always best, 'less you can catch a new one that's fit to make an old one out of.

Sarah Orne Jewett

••

....

The ideal of friendship is to feel as one while remaining two.

Madame Swetchine

....

A FRIEND

A friend sees the best in you, even when you're not showing it.

A friend knows when you need someone to talk to, when you need to be alone, and, most important, the difference between the two.

A friend can tell when you need a hug, and doesn't hesitate to offer one.

A friend makes you laugh when you see little to laugh about.

A friend will always come to your defense, no matter how often called upon to do it or how unpopular it makes her or him.

A friend believes you first and rumors second.

A friend never passes up the chance to encourage you.

A friend shares with you, even chocolate.

A friend tells you when you're about to make a mistake.

A friend is someone you can always depend on, even when you don't deserve it.

A friend brings out the best in you, but doesn't insist on the credit.

A friend understands you, even when you don't.

Martha Bolton

....

Only your real friends will tell you when your face is dirty.

Sicilian Proverb

....

My father always used to say that when you die, if you've got five real friends, then you've had a great life.

Lee Iacocca

Don't flatter yourself that friendship authorizes you to say disagreeable things to your intimates. The nearer you come into relation with a person, the more necessary do tact and courtesy become.

Oliver Wendell Holmes

YOU CALLED ME FRIEND

Tolstoy, the great Russian writer, was passing along a street one day when a beggar stopped him and pleaded for alms. The great Russian searched through his pockets for a coin, but finding none he retretfully said, "Please don't be angry with me, my friend, but I have nothing with me. If I did I would gladly give it to you."

The beggar's face flamed up, and with tears in his eyes, he said, "You have given me more than I asked for. You have called me friend."

Author Unknown

Friendships are fragile things and require as much care in handling as any other fragile and precious thing.

Randolph S. Bourne

••

My coat and I live comfortably together. It has assumed all my wrinkles, does not hurt me anywhere, has molded itself to my deformities and is complacent to all my movements. I only feel its presence because it keeps me warm. Old coats and old friends are the same.

Victor Hugo

If you live to be a hundred, I want to live to be a hundred minus one day, so I never have to live without you.

Winnie-the-Pooh

••

DOS AND DON'TS OF FEMININE FELLOWSHIP

*H*ere goes:

Do Follow Up on Promises

If you tell a friend you'll pray for her, really do it! In fact, dropping your friend a postcard in the mail on the day you remember her in prayer might be just the encouragement she needs!

Do Learn the Art of Listening

Body language says a lot. Are you listening with your eyes as well as your ears? Also, make sure you don't respond to every comment by saying, "You know, the exact same thing happened to me," and turning the conversation to your issues. Instead, ask follow-up questions to learn more about your friend and her situation, and demonstrate interest in what she's telling you.

Do Celebrate Your Friend's Happiness and Success
Did your friend just get a promotion at work? Find out she's pregnant? Lose fifteen pounds? Let her know you're thrilled when she experiences the good things life has to offer. If you let jealousy or competition keep you from celebrating with your friends, you may find yourself alone, with no one who cares about your good news when the tide turns and your ship comes in.

Do Love Your Friend Enough to Tell Her the Truth
If a friend asks you if a bathing suit makes her look like a boat, you might want to refrain from asking if she means houseboat or cruise ship. At the same time, if the suit she's picked is the least flattering of the bunch, she'll appreciate your diplomatic attempt to steer her toward a better option.

It's tempting to want to tell people what we think they want to hear, but the very best friends care enough to tell the truth. Do I have lipstick on my teeth? *Yes.* I had this big fight with my husband last night—do you think I overreacted and should apologize? *From what you told me, you definitely owe him dinner and roses.* Does this dress make me look fat? *You've got a nice waistline. Let's see if we can find something that shows it off better.* You get the idea.

Do Be an Encourager
Beyond our front doors, life's a jungle. It can be a jungle this side of the front door too. You know what can make all the difference in the world? An encouraging word from someone who really cares about us. Did your friend tell you she wants to lose weight? Improve her marriage? Stop smoking? Get her head on straight? Reorganize her pantry? Beat breast cancer? Survive this divorce? Climb out of her depression? Get on track with God?

Let her know you believe in her.

The words "You can do this" mean a lot.

The words "I'll be there to encourage you any way I can" mean even more.

And the phrase "You know, it's Jesus who can give us the strength to accomplish even the toughest things in life—I'll be praying for your relationship with Him" might mean the most of all.

Don't Hide Behind a Façade of Perfection or Control

Vulnerability says a lot. Do you trust your friend enough to tell her the truth about struggles or imperfections in your life? If not, she probably won't feel comfortable confiding in you either.

Don't Tell Secrets!

Mum's the word. If a friend shares something confidential, don't disclose her secret—no matter how juicy it is!

Don't Try to Have an Answer for Everything

Sometimes, in the face of a friend's deep pain, there are no answers that will suffice. Holding a hand, hugging a shoulder, or shedding tears together may be better options.

Karen Scalf Linamen

• •

A real friend never gets in the way, unless you happen to be on the way down.
Evan Esar

• •

HELLO FROM HEAVEN

When the phone rang at 11:30 P.M. I always knew who was calling. "Hi, Berniece," I'd say. We had a routine, Berniece and I. She was my closest friend for 30 years, and we called each other every night. I couldn't remember exactly when we met, because I felt like I had always known her. So on a night in 1990 when the phone rang at 11:30, I reached for the receiver out of habit. But I hadn't spoken to Berniece for several days. She was in intensive care.

"Roberta!" said the sweet voice on the other end. There was no question. It was my friend. She sounded well and strong. I couldn't believe my ears.

Berniece and I lived nearby and we often got together, but the phone was our way of winding down after the three-to-eleven shift at our jobs. I was a proofreader for a publishing company, and Berniece worked at the Western Electric plant. Our houses were quiet when we got home, with our families fast asleep. I got in around 11:15, fixed a cup of tea, and sat by the phone. Some nights I'd call, and others I'd just wait for it to ring. "Thank God for telephones, right?" I said once. Berniece chuckled. Her job was assembling them down at the plant.

We had lots of laughs in those late-night calls. We prayed together too. Having Berniece on the phone was like having a direct line to heaven. She had a powerful faith, and she bolstered mine. Mostly we talked about our children. I had one son, but Berniece had a houseful—five children she'd embraced when she married their dad. I worried the marriage would never work out. "Love is the answer," Berniece said. "You'll see." For her, love was always the answer. Their home became one of the happiest I'd ever seen. She welcomed people at the door with a grin. "Just in time for cake," she'd say. Even with her job and the children, she made marvels in the kitchen. Many times I'd hear a knock, and it would be her daughter Tina: "Mom made too much chili. Here's some for you." Berniece knew I was crazy about her chili.

The main topic of conversation in our late-night calls continued to be our children as we struggled through their growing-up years. "Let's pray," she said one night. "God understands teenagers better than we do."

Eventually Berniece had to give up her job because her health was failing. She had diabetes, and problems with her heart. She still called to chat at 11:30, but her voice was often weak.

When she was taken to the hospital in 1990 I wasn't able to see her. I was still working, and visiting hours were limited. But Tina kept me posted. "She promises to get well," Tina told me one day. "And she sends her love." Love was always the answer for Berniece.

Dear God, make her well again. Your love is the answer.

A few days later, Tina called, sounding worried. "Mom's getting worse," she said. That night I was thinking of Berniece and the phone rang at 11:30. Just like old times. "Berniece!" I said. "How are you?"

"You should see this!" she said. "An angel is smiling at me. An angel dressed in magenta and gold, his wings reaching the ceiling." I couldn't find words. My friend sounded so strong and excited. "Another angel is dressed in blue. They are so beautiful! I feel so good, Roberta. I'll be home in the morning." She hung up. Angels with Berniece, how perfect. And how like Berniece to want to share the vision with her best friend.

I slept soundly and woke with joy in my heart. There was a knock at my door. It was Tina. I pulled her inside. I blurted out about Berniece's call. "It couldn't be," Tina said quietly. "Mom died in her sleep last night. Around eleven-thirty."

It couldn't be, but it was true. God had healed Berniece, and she was home, just as she'd said she would be. My phone had rung with a message from my friend, direct from heaven.

Roberta Ley

THE POWER OF POPCORN

I crept up to the door and knocked.

I was scared—just a little—but far too excited to pay the fear much attention.

A gruff voice bellowed (just another part of the routine), "Who is it?"

Quietly, I whispered, "It's Nancy, Mr. Hoag."

"What do you want?" he yelled. (As if he doesn't already know.)

Larger than life is the image that approached the back door. His low, raspy voice bellowed out of his warm, smiling face. A smile is all I needed! I am instantly reassured and feel welcomed. In a matter of seconds, I lead my gang of four or five neighborhood kids and two brothers through the house to the living room.

There it was—the complete set-up. Two chairs, facing each other, on either side of the square iron floor register. In the center of the register sat a huge, enamel wash basin filled to the rim with fresh hot popcorn.

Mr. Hoag knew the way to my heart was through my nose!

I was the undisputed most dedicated popcorn lover of the whole group of kids living on the hill. The aroma filled the air and caused a magnetic attraction . . . kids and snacks, a natural combination. There was no better smell on earth than Mr. Hoag's home-grown, fluffy, white kernel popcorn. On a little wooden stool sat a stack of white paper bags.

One by one, we took our turn sitting on the chair opposite this grand man, chatting with him while he fills our bag.

He listened to each one of us with great interest. Whether we told him our troubles or victories, he listened intently. Our words were important to him. Our opinions mattered to him. He never made fun of us or what we told him. He said few words, but we knew we were valued and worthy of this man's attention. After all, he took the time to make us popcorn and to listen.

We each gave him a heartfelt thank you and a warm hug, even the boys did! Well, except for John and Joey. They were the older ones, and Mr. Hoag acknowledged their "big-boy" status with a handshake.

On the couch, at the other end of the living room was his beautiful wife, grinning as she watched the parade. Although they had no children of their own, Mrs. Hoag, an English teacher at my school, and Mr. Hoag were child-friendly folks. They loved us and we could feel it. Cared for and strengthened, we confidently ran off, treats in hand.

I'm not sure what we loved more . . . the popcorn, or Mr. Hoag! I do know that I was a scapegoat for my peers at school, with their childish and often painful pranks. My parents loved me and suffered when I came home crying from school. They told me of my worth and encouraged me as best they could. But, typical of a child, I thought they had to say all that!

They were my Mom and Dad and had to love me.

So, heavenly backup was provided and my self-esteem was restored nightly, by a seventy-five-year-old, ornery, teddy bear who knew the power of popcorn. He used that delicious treat to show how he cared for not only me, but for all the neighborhood kids.

I am so thankful that this wonderful man took the time and effort to make a difference in our lives.

Showing interest, acceptance, and love took so little time. But the effects will be with us for a lifetime and with our children, too.

Nancy Eckerson

THE BAKER'S DAUGHTER

Oh, but the Baker's Daughter is beautiful!

The Baker's Daughter has yellow hair, and every night it is curled with rags, and every morning it stands out in a frizzy fluff round her head. The Baker's Daughter has blue dresses and pink dresses and spotted dresses with flounces and flounces on them; she has beads around her neck and jingly bracelets and a ring with a real stone. All the girls in class sigh with envy of the Baker's Daughter.

But the Baker's Daughter is proud. She points her chin and she turns up her nose, and she is very, very superior. You never see her in the Baker's shop. She strolls up and down the sidewalk, sucking her beads.

You all know the Baker's shop, two steps down. It is warm in there, and busy. It smells of hot bread, and every few minutes the Baker, a hot, untidy little man in shirt sleeves, comes up from the basement carrying a big tray of crullers, or shiny rolls, or twisted currant buns. The Baker works hard all day and he never has time to do more than just poke his nose outside the doorway, every hour or so, for a sniff of cool air. It is hard to believe that anything so beautiful as the Baker's Daughter could ever come out of the Baker's shop!

Once I started to write a poem. It began:

> Oh, it is the Baker's Daughter,
> And she is grown so fair, so fair . . .

I thought I would make a very splendid valentine of it, all written out in a fine hand, with pink roses around and lots of crinkly paper lace, and send it to her, secretly. But unfortunately I found out that it was too much like a poem that someone else wrote a long time ago, and so I have never finished it. But still it always comes into my mind whenever I see the Baker's Daughter sucking her beads.

There was only one thing in the Baker's shop that at all

came up in magnificence to the Baker's Daughter herself, and that was the big round cake that sat in the place of honor, right in the middle of the Baker's window. It was a chocolate cake, with all sorts of twirls and twiddles of lovely icing on it, and the word BIRTHDAY written in pink sugar letters. For some reason or other the Baker would never sell that cake. Perhaps he was afraid he would never be able to make another one quite so beautiful. He would sell you any other cake from his window but that one, and even if you went there very early of a Friday morning, which is cruller day, when there are no cakes at all, and asked him for a nice party cake, he would say:

"I can let you have one by three o'clock!"

And if you then asked: "But how about the cake in the window?" he would reply:

"That's not for sale. You can have one by three o'clock!"

For though you should offer him dollars and dollars, he would never sell that cake!

I seldom dare to speak to the Baker's Daughter. I am much too humble. But still she has friends. Never little boys; these she points her chin at, from across the street. But there are little girls with whom she is on friendly terms for as much as a week at a time. Naturally they are very proud. If you can't be a princess or a movie star, perhaps the next best thing is to be seen walking up to the drug store soda fountain with the Baker's Daughter, and sitting there beside her on a tall stool eating a pineapple sundae.

Now there was one little girl with whom the Baker's Daughter condescended at one time to be friends. Perhaps her name had something to do with it. She was called Carmelita Miggs, and Carmelita is a very romantic and superior name. She had black hair and a pair of bronze slippers, and she was the only little girl ever seen to stroll publicly with the Baker's Daughter, arm in arm. What they talked about no one knew. But Carmelita sometimes wore the Baker's Daughter's beads, and the Baker's Daughter would wear Carmelita's beads, and altogether they were very, very special friends while it lasted.

And it lasted until Carmelita had a birthday party.

The Baker's Daughter of course was invited, and several other of Carmelita's school friends. It was to be a real party, at four in the afternoon, with ice cream. And the Baker's Daughter said, very grandly, that she would bring a cake.

"I will bake you a nice one," said her father, "with orange icing on it. Now let me see . . . how many of you will there be?"

But that wasn't at all what the Baker's Daughter wanted. Anyone at all could bring a cake with orange icing. *I will choose my own cake!* thought the Baker's Daughter.

But all she said was: "That will be very nice!"

And in the afternoon, while her father was down in the bake-shop kitchen putting the last twiddle on the orange cake (for he wanted to make it something very special) and while her mother was taking forty winks in the back parlor, and the bakery cat was sound asleep, with her four paws curled under her, behind the counter, the Baker's Daughter crept into the shop on tiptoe, in all her finery, and stole—yes, *stole*—that big magnificent cake from the very middle of the shop window!

You see, she had had her eye on it, all along!

Oh, but she looked proud, walking down the street with that big cake in her arms! Everyone turned to look at her.

She lifted it up—and a nice, light cake it seemed—wooden platter and all, and she covered it over with sheets of waxy paper and carried it round to Carmelita's house.

Oh, but she looked proud, walking down the street with that big cake in her arms! Everyone turned to look at her.

"What a lovely cake!" cried all the little boys and girls when she arrived at Carmelita's house.

And the wrappings were taken off, very carefully, and it

was set right in the middle of the table, with candles all around it.

"*What* a nice, light cake!" said Carmelita's mother.

"All good cakes are light!" said the Baker's Daughter.

"It was very, very kind of your father to make such a splendid cake," said Carmelita's mother.

"I chose it myself!" said the Baker's Daughter, tossing her head.

They talked a little, very politely, and Carmelita Miggs showed all her birthday presents. And at last came the moment for the ice cream to be handed round on little glass plates.

"And now," said Carmelita's mother, "we'll all have some of that delicious cake!"

Carmelita had to cut it, because it was her birthday. She stood there feeling very shy, for there was a great silence all round; everyone's eyes were fixed on the cake, and all one could hear was Tommy Bates busily sucking his ice cream spoon, so as to get through first.

Only the Baker's Daughter sat there proudly, with her skirts spread out, looking indifferent, as though cakes like this were quite an everyday affair with her!

Carmelita took the knife and stuck it into the very middle of the pink icing, and pushed. You could have heard a pin drop.

But the knife didn't go in. Carmelita turned very red, and took a long breath and tried again.

Still the knife wouldn't go in.

"You must try harder, dear," said Carmelita's mother, smiling pleasantly. "I expect the top icing is a little bit stiff! Do you want me to help you?"

Now Carmelita knew that she had been pushing just as hard as she could. It came upon her, all at once, that there must be something very, very queer about that cake! But she took another long breath, again, and this time her mother put *her* hand on the knife, too.

You could have heard *two* pins drop!

And then, suddenly, there was a funny "plop," and the knife went in. And as it went in the cake slipped and turned a sort of somersault, and there it was, upside down, sticking on the tip of the knife that Carmelita's mother was still holding, and everyone looking most surprised. And that wasn't the worst of it!

It was all hollow inside!

In fact, it was just a big pasteboard shell covered over with icing, and *that* was why the Baker would never sell it to anyone!

Can you imagine how the party felt? How the little boys and girls whispered and giggled, how Carmelita wept and the Baker's Daughter grew redder and redder, and snifflier and snifflier, and how Carmelita's mother tried to smooth everything over and pretend that it was really all very funny, and quite the nicest thing that could happen at any birthday party? And how, at the very last minute, while the ice cream was all melting away, they had to send out and buy a real cake, *somewhere else!*

But Carmelita Miggs didn't think it was a joke. She never, never forgave the Baker's Daughter for spoiling her party. For quite a long time she wouldn't speak to her at all. As for the other boys and girls, whenever they met Carmelita or the Baker's Daughter they would say:

"Now we'll all have some cake!"

You would think, after this, that the Baker's Daughter would have changed her ways. But not a bit of it! I saw her, only the other day, strolling up and down the sidewalk and sucking her beads just as proud as ever.

As I went past her I whispered very softly: "Now we'll all have some cake!"

And do you know what the Baker's Daughter did? I hate to tell you.

She stuck—out—her—tongue!

There, in the middle of the Baker's window, is another cake. This time it has green icing and pink roses, and two little sugar doves on top. It is even grander than the old one, and will probably last twice as long.

Unless, of course, someone else should have a birthday party!

Margery Williams Bianco

· ·

If, instead of a gem, or even a flower, we could cast the gift of a lovely thought into the heart of a friend, that would be giving as the angels give.

George MacDonald

· ·

FOREVER FRIEND

Sometimes in life, you find a special friend;
Someone who changes your life by being a part of it.
Someone who makes you laugh until you can't stop;
Someone who makes you believe that there is really
      good in this world.
Someone who convinces you that there is
An unlocked door just waiting for you to open it.
This is Forever Friendship.

When you're down, and the world seems dark and
      empty,
Your Forever Friend lifts you up in spirit

And makes that dark and empty world suddenly seem
    bright and full.
Your Forever Friend gets you through the hard times,
And the sad times, and the confused times.

If you turn and walk away your Forever Friend follows.
If you lose your way, your Forever Friend guides you
    and cheers you on.

Your Forever Friend holds your hand
And tells you that everything is going to be a-okay.
And when you find such a Friend, you'll feel happy and
    complete,
Because you need not worry.

You Have A "Forever Friend" for Life
And Forever Has No End. . .

Laurieann Kelly

FRIENDS AND FLOWERS

Dottie was in her seventies and an avid gardener. She had a glorious English flower garden in her backyard, with vibrant blooms of all varieties and colors running rampant along her meandering fence. It was breathtaking just to step out of her back door and into her botanical kingdom—a reflection of her English heritage.

I, in contrast, don't have a green thumb (or any other digit) on my body. All I have to do is *look* at our plants and they seem to wither up and die before our very eyes. If plants could talk, they would scream, "Oh no! Please don't leave us here with *her*!" Sigh.

Dottie to the rescue! She called one day (imagine an Australian accent) and said, "Mary, this is Dottie. Now, I just wondered if you and Charlotte (my best friend with whom I share a house) would allow me to come out to your house and plant a few flowers in your yard? I have some beautiful purple iris that I think would be pretty along your back fence."

"Oh, Dottie, we would be *thrilled* if you did that. And purple is one of my favorite colors."

"Well, good then. One day soon I'll give you a ring and just pop over and plant a few bulbs for you."

"Wonderful, Dottie! And thanks for thinking of us. I know Charlotte will be excited too."

A few days later, I looked out the back window, and there was Dottie on her hands and knees in our backyard, digging holes in the dirt and planting iris bulbs along the fence. She stayed for about an hour, planting and watering. And the next time I looked out, she was gone. She was like the phantom flower fairy godmother. Zap! And purple iris sprang up all along our fence.

Fortunately for me (since I'm botanically dysfunctional), iris are perennial flowers. That means they come back up every year, because God takes care of them . . . not me. Thank you, God. So every year in April, purple iris spring back up in our backyard. And every year we thank Dottie for them again, because they are like a new gift each year.

A couple of years after Dottie planted the iris for us, one Sunday she came up to us at church. The sister churches in our fellowship were having a county-wide meeting in downtown Fort Worth at the convention center, and Dottie wanted to go, but she was afraid to drive into town by herself at night. She asked us if she could go with us. We told her we would be happy for her to go with us, but we had come to church in Charlotte's two-door, two-seat sports car; so there wasn't room for all of us. She said we could take her car, if I would drive. So we agreed.

We got in her car, and I adjusted the seat. Then I put the

key in and . . . stopped. I sat there for a moment just taking in her dashboard. There were little sticky notes everywhere, telling Dottie what to do with various buttons, levers, and knobs. I was astounded.

One note said, "Blue light? Press right." I finally figured out that it meant when the blue light came on, indicating her headlights were on high, she should press the lever to the right to turn off the blue light and lower the headlights. *Interesting*, I thought.

Another note said, "When on E, feed me." *Hmmm*, I wondered. *When on E, feed me. What in the world?* And then it came to me—when the gas gauge showed "E" for empty, she was supposed to feed (fill up) the car with gas." I chuckled to myself on that one. *Weird, but if it works for Dottie, why not?*

It was the third note that really stumped me, though. It said simply, "Breathe." *Breathe? Breathe!* I noodled on that one for quite a while, but I just couldn't figure it out. Why would anyone need to be reminded to breathe? And if they did need to be reminded to breathe, should they be driving? *Strange.*

We enjoyed the church meeting and then returned to the church building where we picked up Charlotte's car. Dottie only lived a few blocks from the church; so I drove her car home, and Charlotte followed us in hers.

On the way home from Dottie's we laughed about the sticky notes on the dash and tried to figure out what the one that read "breathe" meant. We never came up with a satisfactory answer.

A few weeks later, we began to notice that Dottie seemed to be slipping a little mentally. She couldn't remember people's names—people she had known for many years. She couldn't remember how to get home from the church building, even though she had always been famous for her incredible sense of direction. Her clothes, which had always been perfectly matched and impeccable, were sometimes wrinkled and unkempt . . . and sometimes mismatched. That was just not like Dottie at all. So we called her daughter to ask if her children had noticed what was happening.

"Well, yes," said her daughter. "I guess Mom hasn't told you, has she?"

"Told us what?" asked Charlotte.

"Mom has Alzheimer's disease," she said, "and she's had it for some time. It's advancing rather quickly, I'm afraid."

"Oh, I'm so sorry; we didn't know," said Charlotte.

Within a few weeks Dottie had been relocated to a top-notch Alzheimer's center in Fort Worth. And once in a while we would take our church choir, with whom Dottie had sung for many years, to the center to sing for her and her fellow patients. Most of the time she didn't know who we were anymore, but she always remembered the songs, and she would come and stand with us and sing with all her heart. It was a bittersweet time for us.

We lost Dottie in the fall, and our choir sang for her funeral. It was a wonderful celebration with a touch of sadness and loss.

While thinking of Dottie and reading up on Alzheimer's disease a few days later, I made an interesting discovery. Alzheimer's patients often die because they suffocate—their brains forget to tell their bodies to . . . breathe. Suddenly the sticky-note mystery was solved.

Now, ten years later, every spring we are beautifully reminded of our sweet friend Dottie when glorious purpose iris spring up along the fence in our backyard. And we rejoice that she is, no doubt, happily on her hands and knees in heaven's garden, digging in the dirt and planting flowers for everyone to enjoy—perennials that God . . . and Dottie . . . take care of year after year.

Mary Hollingsworth

IF I SHOULD DIE BEFORE I WAKE . . .
CALL MY FRIEND

Peggy knows exactly what to do if I should die suddenly. She has her orders! Before my body is cold, she's supposed to nose around, see that I've left this earth in an orderly fashion, and take care of anything that might be left undone.

For instance, I'd want her to make sure there's nothing disgusting growing in my refrigerator, like rotten lettuce or moldy cheese, unless by chance I'm in the middle of an experiment like maybe growing my own penicillin.

Peggy would know instinctively that I wouldn't want a dirty cup or glass in the sink, and she'd know to slice a lemon and run it through the disposal to give it a fresh smell. If they should carry me out feet first and the bed wasn't made, she would make it.

I'd want her to look around for anything that might embarrass me, like the dirt under the big kitchen rug. When I cook I kick crumbs and crud under it to be dealt with at a later time. Often a much later time! She knows about the mouse traps in the bread drawer and would know to remove them so as not to encourage those gossipy types who would say, "I've heard she had you-know-what's in her you-know-where. If that's not crazy, I don't know what is."

There's a perfectly logical explanation for the you-know-whats in the you-know-where! Several years ago we discovered telltale traces of mice in our bread drawer. We spoke to our two cats about it and they assured us (mostly by their blank looks) that had these sneaky little rodents set foot in their kitchen, they would have known about it and acted immediately, if not sooner. From that we concluded the mice had "broken and entered" through the back of the bread drawer.

With an "I'll fix them," I headed straight to the hardware store, bought traps, and put them in the bread drawer. I intended to go back later and set them. (Would you leave your mouse traps sitting out in plain sight? I don't think so.) Perhaps just the sight of the traps scared the mice back into the woods. I never set the traps and never saw the mouse mess again.

Thank heaven for Peggy. She would fix things and I could rest in peace, knowing I'd covered all my bases here on earth. Having my bases covered for the hereafter is quite another thing! I'm thankful that God didn't have to make arrangements as elaborate as mine when he planned for our eternal destiny. He only asked us to accept that his Son Jesus paid the consequences for our sin and to live our lives in gratitude and obedience. What could be simpler?

Sue Buchanan

••

Friendship is the inexpressible comfort of feeling safe with a person, having neither to weigh thoughts nor measure words.
George Eliot

••

COME AGAIN SOON

Your letter came today amidst magazines, circulars and bills, and my heart tripped over itself in anticipation. I purposely tucked it on the bottom of the stack, saving the best for last. When finally I came to the happy yellow envelope, I paused. I went to the kitchen and fixed myself a cup of tea, then curled up in my favorite chair on the sun porch to savor every word.

It was almost like having you there with me, for we had sat talking on that porch so often before you moved away. I could hear your voice and see your laughing brown eyes. You teased me gently as always and counseled me with your quiet wisdom. You bared your troubled soul and shared your joyful heart.

So, it was with a sigh of contentment and a sense of remorse that I came to the familiar "I love you" at the end. I sat quietly for several minutes, sipping my tea, remembering . . . wishing. Please come again soon, friend. I miss you.

Mary Hollingsworth

•••

Laughter is not a bad beginning for a friendshhip, and it is the best ending for one.

Oscar Wilde

•••

Acknowledgments

All material that originally appeared in *Daily Guideposts* and *Guideposts* magazine is reprinted with permission. Copyright ©1991, 1994, 1997, 2001 by Guideposts, Carmel, New York 10512. All rights reserved.

A Smile Increases Your Face Value. Lombard, IL: Great Quotations, 1990.

Angus, Fay. *Running Around in Spiritual Circles*. San Francisco: Harper, 1986.

Beard, Zarette. "Keep Your Lights Off." Used by permission. ZaretteBeard@yahoo.com.

Boswell, Barbara. Excerpted from *Every Time I Turn Around I Bump Into God*. WinePress Publishing © 2003. Used by permission of the author who may be reached at www.barbboswell.com or bbos2@juno.com.

Bianco, Margery Williams. "The Baker's Daughter" from *A Street of Little Shops*. New York: Doubleday, 1932.

Bolton, Martha. *Never Ask Delilah for a Trim*. Grand Rapids, MI: Bethany House, a division of Baker Book House, 1998.

————. *I Love You...Still: To Keep the Love, You Gotta Laugh.* Grand Rapids, MI: Fleming Revell, a division of Baker Book House, 2000.

————.*Didn't My Skin Used to Fit?* Grand Rapids, MI: Bethany House, a division of Baker Book House, 2000.

Bosch, Henry G. *Our Daily Bread.* © 1974, 1976. Grand Rapids, MI.: RBC Ministries. Reprinted by permission. All rights reserved.

Branch, Susan. *Girlfriends Forever.* New York: Little, Brown &Co., 2001.

Brilliant, Ashleigh. "Pot Shots." Copyright by Ashleigh Brilliant. Used by permission. www.ashleighbrilliant.com.

Buchanan, Sue. *Duh-Votions.* Copyright © 1999 by Sue Buchanan. Used by permission of The Zondervan Corporation.

Calkin, Ruth Harms. "Special Friendships." Used by permission.

————. "Unforgiveness." Used by permission.

Taken from : *Who Put My Life on Fast-Forward?* Copyright © 2002 by Phil Callaway. Published by Harvest House Publishers, Eugene, OR. www.harvesthousepublishers.com. Used by Permission.

Taken from *Best Devotions of Patsy Clairmont* by Patsy Clairmont. Copyright © 2001 by Women of Faith. Used by permission of The Zondervan Corporation.

Eckerson, Nancy Jo. "The Power of Popcorn." Copyright © 1996. Used by permission. For more information on this or other stories by author, please contact folknanc@yahoo.com.

Eller, T. Suzanne. "That's What Friends Do." Used by permission. Suzanne Eller is an author and speaker. She can be reached at tseller@daretobelieve.org.

Taken from: *Coffee Cup Friendship and Cheesecake Fun.* Copyright © 2001 by Becky Freeman. Published by Harvest House Publishers, Eugene, OR. www.harvesthousepublishers.com. Used by permission.

Greeson, Charlotte. "The Nineteen and Half Finger Duet." Used by permission.

Guilmartin, Nance. *Healing Conversations: What to Say When You Don't Know What to Say.* San Francisco: Jossey-Bass, 2002.

Hollingsworth, Amy. *The Simple Faith of Mr. Rogers.* Nashville: Integrity, 2005.

Hollingsworth, Mary. Administered by Shady Oaks Studio, 1507 Shirley Way, Bedford, TX 76022. Used by permission.

———. "All Roads Lead to Texarkana." Administered by Shady Oaks Studio, 1507 Shirley Way, Bedford, TX 76022. Used by permission.

———. "To Lament or Laugh." Administered by Shady Oaks Studio, 1507 Shirley Way, Bedford, TX 76022. Used by permission.

———. "Friends or Sisters?" Administered by Shady Oaks Studio, 1507 Shirley Way, Bedford, TX 76022. Used by permission.

Holmes, Marjorie. *Love and Laughter.* New York: Bantam, a division of Random House, Inc., 1967.

Taken from *Joy Breaks* by Barbara E. Johnson, Patsy Clairmont, Luci Swindoll, Marilyn Meberg. Copyright © 1997 by New Life Clinics. Used by permission of The Zondervan Corporation.

Johnson, Barbara. *Fresh Elastic for Stretched out Moms.* Grand Rapids, MI: Baker Book House, 2003.

Reprinted from *When Perfect Isn't Enough.* Copyright © 2003 by Nancy Kennedy. Used by permission of WaterBrook Press, Colorado Springs, CO. All rights reserved.

Linamen, Karen Scalf. *Just Hand Over the Chocolate and No One Will Get Hurt.* Grand Rapids: Fleming H. Revell, a division of Baker Publishing Group, 1999.

———. *Welcome to the Funny Farm.* Grand Rapids: Fleming H. Revell, a division of Baker Publishing Group, 2001.

———. *I'm Not Suffering From Insanity—I'm Enjoying Every Minute of It.* Grand Rapids: Fleming H. Revell, a division of Baker Publishing Group, 2002.

Reprinted from *101 Simple Lessons for Life.* Copyright © 2003 by Marsha Marks. Used by permission of WaterBrook Press, Colorado Springs, CO. All rights reserved.

The late Dr. Bruce McIver, *Stories I Couldn't Tell While I was a Pastor.* Dallas, TX: Word, 1991. Used by permission.

McPherson, John. *Close to Home.* Used by permission.

Ohrbach, Barbara Milo. *All Things Are Possible.* New York: Crown, a division of Random House, 1995.

Phillips, Bob. *The World's Greatest Collection of Clean Jokes.* Eugene, OR: Harvest House, 1998. Used by permission. www.harvesthousepublishers.com.

———. *Bob Phillip's Encyclopedia of Good Clean Jokes.* Copyright © 1992 by Harvest House Publishers. Published by Harvest House Publishers, Eugene, OR. www.harvesthousepublishers.com. Used by Permission.

———. *Phillip's Book of Great Thoughts and Funny Sayings.* Wheaton, IL: Tyndale, 1993.

© 2003 by Rhonda Rhea. *Amusing Grace.* Used with permission by Cook Communications Ministries. To order, www.cookministries.com. All rights reserved.

St. John-Gilbert, Rachel. *Wake Up Laughing.* Uhrichsville, OH: Barbour, 2003. Used by permission.

© 2001 by Stan Toler. *The Buzzards Are Circling But God Isn't Finished with Me Yet.* Used with permission by Cook Communications Ministries. To order, www.cookministries.com. All rights reserved.

Walker, Laura Jensen. *Through the Rocky Road and Into the Rainbow Sherbet: Hope and Laughter for Life's Hard Licks.* Grand Rapids, MI: Fleming Revell, a division of Baker Publishing Group, 2002.

Ron Wheeler. Used by permission. www.cartoonworks.com.

Wright, Rusty and Linda Raney. *500 Clean Jokes and Humorous Stories* published by Barbour Publishing, Inc. Uhrichsville, OH: Barbour, 1985. Used by permission.

Youngman, Henny. *The Encyclopedia of One Liners by Henny Youngman.* Katonah, NY: Ballymote, 1989.